you and your GERMAN SHEPHERD PUPPY

in a nutshell

The essential owners' guide to perfect puppy parenting – with easy-to-follow steps on how to choose and care for your new arrival

Carry Aylward

NUTSHELL BOOKS

Front cover design by Nutshell Books
Book design by Nutshell Books
Photography: SashaFoxWalters, © AdobeStock, © Colourbox, Carry Aylward, © Shutterstock, © iStock

Printed by Kindle Direct Publishing

First printed 2019

Nutshell Books
3 Holmlea Road, Goring on Thames
RG8 9EX, United Kingdom
www.nutshell-books.com

*To all the German Shepherds that enrich
our lives, and especially:*

- *Zena, who guarded me in my pram
  and stayed by my side when I learned
  to walk,*

- *Ascii, who did the
  same for my own
  children, and*

- *Arco, always ready
  to help.*

CONTENTS

FOREWORD

So you're thinking of sharing your life with a German Shepherd – undisputed hero and king of dogs? And you're considering a puppy at that!

Let's flash forward to the scene, to the ears straight up, funnelled towards you, following your every sound. To the bright eyes assessing and predicting your every move; head tilting to one side, then the other, weighing up your every thought. Yup, every fluffy hair on his being is keenly alert and ready for action. You're locked into his radar and he's got you absolutely sussed. So if you're wanting to invite a German Shepherd into your home you'll need to get your act together too.

It's a daunting venture, no question, but also one that is hugely, wonderfully exciting. Hats off to you for considering a puppy from the world's most revered and heroic dog breed. And whether or not you've had a German Shepherd before, congratulations on taking this step to being or becoming the best puppy parent you can be.

Of course, there's no getting a German Shepherd into a 'nutshell' – there's far too much to these noble and majestic dogs. (Figuratively speaking, any German Shepherd in its rightful place is better suited to a pedestal.) What this book does offer in a nutshell is the most up-to-date, practical advice for new, or out-of-practice, owners on choosing and raising a German Shepherd puppy.

The book flows chronologically, from the decision to invite a German Shepherd into your life, to finding a litter, choosing your puppy, and preparing for the big homecoming. It then guides you on picking up your new family member, and walks you step by step through the vital first days, weeks and months. This timeline structure necessitates some repetition and cross-referencing, but this is in case, going forward, you choose to re-visit certain sections in isolation.

The format is concise and easy to read. Simple-to-follow DOs and DON'Ts make important information quickly and easily accessible – because there are things you shouldn't wait to find out only once you have the time for more in-depth study. The first months of your puppy's life largely shape the dog he will grow into, and THIS is when you need to put the most energy into his upbringing and training.

Also for the sake of easy reading, your puppy is referred to as 'he'. To use 'he or she' throughout would be clumsy, and 'it' feels blatantly impersonal, so please consider 'he' to mean 'she or he' in every instance.

While the upcoming advice is intended to help you build a solid foundation for a wonderful relationship with your German Shepherd, nothing can truly prepare you for the first few months. They will be a rollercoaster ride of pure exhilaration and hair-pulling frustration. You will gain love and laughter by the barrel, and you will lose valued possessions and a few night's sleep. There will be flashes of obedience and pure genius from your puppy, and they will be matched with slip-up moments that have your head spinning with horror. Come what may, you'll need to strap yourself in for this adventure of a very precious lifetime.

1. ARE YOU READY?

German Shepherds aside for a moment, are you truly ready for a dog? Any dog? Because in all seriousness being a dog owner is no whirlwind ride at the funfair. It's a momentous, life-changing and long-term decision!

If you are new to owning a dog, when you invite one into your world, your life will never be the same. You will soon start thinking differently about what you wear, the places you visit, your holiday destinations, the car you drive and, yes, even your next house. Your life will also be warmer, stinkier, happier … richer in so many ways.

If you invite a dog into your home, he should be treated like family. Ask yourself very honestly whether, at this time in your life, and for the next ten to eleven years, you will be able to give him:

- the love,
- the time,
- the money,
- the space,
- the exercise,
- the care,
- the training
- and the patience

he needs and deserves?

Because **no** dog should ever be cast aside like a pair of shoes its owner has grown tired of.

Is a puppy right for you?

Ask yourself honestly whether you can face the puppy stage with the pooping, weeing and chewing of everything in sight. And whether you have the time. If not, you might consider taking on a dog that has finished with toilet training, teething and even adolescence. It's not unusual for prospective German Shepherd owners to find a highly trained, high-quality adult, and this option is one that could save you hours of hard work.

Another option is to contact an established and reputable breeder to find out if you can give an ex-breeding dog the chance to live as a pet, or take on a dog that hasn't performed as well as expected in the show ring.

Do you value the quiet life?

Have you considered giving a home to a dog in its senior years? If you can find one, there is little more rewarding than taking on a retired working German Shepherd. But there are many beautiful older dogs that need re-homing through no fault of their own, so if you are no longer as active as you once were, this might be the best choice for you now.

An older dog is likely to take longer to adjust than a puppy but as long as he has been treated well, a German Shepherd will soon love you as his ever-own, no matter how old he is when he becomes yours.

Do you have other pets?

If you have other dogs or cats, consider carefully how a new dog would fit in to your family. If you get your German Shepherd as a puppy, there's no reason for him to be a problem with your other pets. Your other pets, however, might not be quite so adaptable.

You still want a puppy?

I know. They're warm and cuddly and there's nothing as sweet as the pitter patter of puppy feet. But the first steps to getting a puppy are a big investment – not just financially, but also in terms of time, energy and emotion. This is not an effort to put you off getting a dog. Quite the opposite. It's just really important that you are sure you are able to give your puppy the happy life it deserves and fully understand the commitment you're making. Too many dogs are re-homed and even put down each year because their owners underestimated the responsibility.

In a nutshell

If you're sure you can give your dog the love and attention he needs and deserves; and you're sure a puppy is the way forward; and you're brave enough to let those four extra feet bound freely through your heart-space, then let's look more closely at the specifics of taking on a German Shepherd.

2. IS A GERMAN SHEPHERD RIGHT FOR YOU?

You're already drawn to the breed or you wouldn't be reading this, but is a German Shepherd right for you? And, just as importantly, are you and your circumstances right for a German Shepherd?

There's a great deal to these dogs – in my somewhat biased opinion more than to other breeds. They are exceptionally grand and noble.

- Physically: they are beautiful, sleek, powerful, athletic, full of energy, and they move with agility, grace and purpose.
- Mentally: they are alert, intelligent, curious, insightful, intuitive.
- Emotionally: they are good-natured, loving, devoted, caring, sensitive and unwaveringly loyal.
- Temperament-wise: they are calm, courageous, fearless and capable.

And the list goes on.

Majestic

> *'A German Shepherd does not go walkies.*
> *A German Shepherd marches out'*
> *Unknown*

One of the first things you're likely to notice in a German Shepherd is his stately air. These dogs give off a nobility and majesty that is rightly due one of the most intelligent, hardworking and agile breeds in the world. Carrying their long necks raised when alert, and lowered on the move, they wear a firm and quiet energy that makes them self-assured without being overbearing; strong and fearless without being hostile or aggressive.

Heroic

The German Shepherd is consistently in the top five most popular registered breeds in the world, and with good reason. No other breed has helped so many people in so many ways. These dogs are heroes in life, just as they are in fiction and film (see the chapter 'Standout German Shepherds' for examples).

Versatile

> *'... dogdom's finest all-purpose workers'*
>
> *AKC*

Max von Stephanitz, who is credited with developing the breed, believed 'utility' to be the 'true criterion of beauty' and, according to the American Kennel Club (AKC), he clearly achieved his purpose.

So these dogs were bred to be useful – originally as herding dogs. But the traits that make German Shepherds fiercely devoted protectors and excellent herders have led them to become the world's top military dog, top guard dog and top police dog. Their exceptional sense of smell and unusual ability to stay focused in busy environments make them invaluable in patrolling troubled areas, tracking down criminals, search and rescue operations, and narcotics and explosives detection missions.

Their devotion makes them reliable disability assistants, and their intelligence has them excelling in obedience classes and starring in films.

As if that's not enough, they also make loving companions and loyal family members.

Intelligent

Research studies indicate that German Shepherds learn and interpret instructions better than almost all other breeds. Reportedly, 95% of the time a typical German Shepherd will obey a simple command the first time he is given it, and will learn simple tasks after just five repetitions.

Intuitive

German Shepherd owners will tell you that their dogs are mind readers – that there's no pulling the wool over their eyes with words that don't hold true to their real motives, thoughts and feelings (other people's as well as their own). In fact, the breed's inbuilt fraud-detector is so well tuned that many owners trust their dog's instincts to the point of welcoming the people the warms to, and being wary of anyone he mistrusts.

Wonderful companions

German Shepherds are a popular breed because they make such faithful protectors and loving companions … because they have all the qualities you'd like in a best friend. There are plenty of sayings about the world being a better place if people were more like dogs. Well, if people were more like German Shepherds the world would be filled with head-tilting mindfulness and intelligence. It would enjoy far more love and far less corruption.

So, what's not to love?

These awesome dogs get gold stars all round, so why on earth wouldn't you choose one?

Shedders

They are shedders, and they have two shed settings:

1. always, and
2. a bit more than always.

If your dog will be indoors and you don't like the idea of hair in your house then a German Shepherd is not right for you.

They generally enjoy being groomed, so getting them to 'Stand' while you brush their coats is unlikely to be a problem, but are YOU ready to give them the regular grooming they need (bi-weekly, if not daily)?

Large

They take up a lot of room! German Shepherds are big dogs, better suited to large houses, and ideally large outdoor areas too, so if your living space is small you might want to reconsider – for his sake and yours.

Also because of their size, there's no scooping them up under one arm if you need more control – not when they're fully grown.

And they are powerful too, so they must be well trained.

Need good training

German Shepherds are always willing to learn new things and eager for a definite purpose, and on top of this, their intelligence needs channelling and nurturing. So, like gifted and talented children, they come with their own challenges. Attention, mental stimulation and training are essential to keep them happy and well-balanced.

Life with a well-trained dog is always more enjoyable, but while for some breeds training is a fun add-on, for German Shepherds it's imperative. If you can't give your dog things to do, he will find things on his own – things that might involve redecorating the furniture for instance. And if that were the case, it would be down to neglect on your part rather than naughtiness on his.

Need proper exercise

While German Shepherds are not dizzyingly hyper-active, their strength and energy need channelling too. They were bred to trot for hours on end, covering great distances, so a short walk around the block won't do. If you have an aversion to exercise, or don't have a huge property for your dog to roam, then a German Shepherd is probably not a good choice for you.

Overprotective

German Shepherds are naturally protective of their owners and, if they have not been socialised properly or have been badly treated, they can become overprotective of their family and territory.

Need an experienced hand

It's important for German Shepherds to understand their place in the 'pack', and also for you, their owner, to be the 'top dog'. They usually have no need to be the alpha dog themselves, but if their owner doesn't assume the role, they could start displaying dominant behaviours which would make them difficult to manage. For this reason, German Shepherds do well with firm handling by gentle but experienced owners, and are not always the best choice for first-time owners.

Weak strains and traits

More than other breeds, German Shepherds are prone to elbow dysplasia and canine hip dysplasia (CHD) which can cause pain in late age and eventually arthritis. Other minor ailments include the Von Willebrand Disease, a hereditary bleeding disorder, and degenerative myelopathy, a neurological disease.

You can minimise the risk by choosing a puppy from a responsibly-bred litter with the relevant health clearance certificates. (See the section: 'Buying responsibly'.)

Bottom line

Just as all German Shepherd puppies have the potential to be great dogs, they all have the potential to be problem children too. Kept caged or locked up for long stretches, they will become 'difficult': barking, digging and chewing things. But if you can give your German Shepherd the love and attention he needs and deserves; if you can keep him active and busy – mentally and physically; and if you can give him playtime, toys and walks, you will have head-tilting love and entertainment beyond measure. And those big, floppy paws will make big, warm paw-prints in your heart.

3. WHAT IS A 'GOOD' GERMAN SHEPHERD?

You've decided you can give a dog the time, care, expense and devotion it needs, and that you want a German Shepherd. I'm thrilled for you. There are wonderful, magical, hilarious, sock-nicking, head-tilting, poo-picking, finger-nipping, chin-licking times ahead. And more love than you could ever imagine.

But, don't rush off to see the first litter you come across – even if you want no more from your German Shepherd than good company. Why? Because it is near impossible to resist the pleading eyes of a puppy that wants to go home with you. Once those eyes have locked onto your heart, they are most likely stuck there for life.

Better to plan ahead. Start doing your research so you can make a wise and informed choice. If it's a pet you're after, you'll be less particular than someone who's looking for a working Shepherd or a show dog. They could all grow into great dogs, but if you don't want to risk weak strains and traits, it's well worth taking the time to track down a breeder whose puppies are a credit to the breed.

Here are some things to understand and consider before you begin your search.

Purebreds

Many puppy farmers and backyard breeders mate their dogs with other breeds, and still advertise them as German Shepherds. Although these puppies might grow into lovely dogs, they are unlikely to have the traits of a true German Shepherd. Again this is up to you, but if you do want a purebred – meaning its parents are of the same breed – it's important that you see both the mother and the father and, if it's not possible to meet the father, that you at least see photos of him or, better still, video footage.

Pedigrees

If you want a pedigree German Shepherd – meaning a purebred dog that is also registered with a recognised and reputable club or society such as the Kennel Club – you must choose a puppy from a breeder who is listed with one of these societies. And if you are planning to show your dog or become a registered breeder yourself, you will certainly need to do more research. The section 'Useful Information' at the end of the book has a list of organisations and websites you can refer to.

But what is a 'good' German Shepherd?

Of course, your dog needn't tick all these boxes to be a great dog or even a great German Shepherd, but it's useful and interesting to know what the breed standard expects.

Temperament is key

- A good German Shepherd has a lovely nature that is ready, willing and eager to help in any way the circumstances dictate: as herder, guide, watchdog, protector or companion.

- His self-confidence – which sometimes comes across as aloofness – is an important trait.
- He is fearless without being hostile – not timid, nervous or shy.
- He is discerning in his friendships – he will quietly stand his ground when approached, and willingly meet overtures without making advances himself.
- His loyalty is incorruptible.

Expression

- He is keen and intelligent, alert and full of life.
- At attention his head is raised and his neck carried high.

Physical appearance

- **Height:** The ideal male measures between 24 and 26 inches (61-66cm) at the wither (the top of the highest point of the shoulder blade), and the ideal female between 22 and 24 inches (56-61cm).
- **Length:** He is longer than he is tall.
- **Outline:** The lines of his body are sleek and smooth rather than angular.
- **Head:** noble and chiselled
- **Eyes:** almond shaped and dark in colour
- **Ears (of an adult dog):** moderately pointed, open towards the front, and carried erect when at attention. Never floppy or hanging
- **Muzzle:** long and strong
- **Nose:** predominantly black
- **Neck:** strong and muscular
- **Chest:** wide and deep
- **Back:** straight and strong, and sloping down from the withers

- **Tail:** bushy and long, low-set and hanging in a slight curve when relaxed. Tails should never be docked. (Docking is the practice of removing a portion of the tail, usually soon after birth.)
- **Coat:** a double coat of medium length. The outer coat is dense, straight and lying close to the body (not silky, woolly or curly). Short hair covers the head, legs and paws, while the neck hair is slightly longer and thicker. (There is more on coat type in the next chapter.)
- **Colour:** most colours are acceptable but strong, rich colours are preferred. Tan with a black saddle is most typical, but according to the breed standard, a good German Shepherd can also be entirely black. White or washed-out colouring is disqualified in the show ring.
- **Impression:** The overall impression he gives is one of strength, fitness and agility. He is solid but not bulky; muscular and lithe, but never spindly.

Movement
- He is co-ordinated and balanced.
- At a walk, a good German Shepherd covers a lot of ground with long strides.
- He is essentially a trotting dog – his gait appears elastic, effortless and rhythmic. His strides are smooth and flowing, close to the ground in a forward rather than upward motion.

Strains of the breed
As a potential buyer, you might be wondering about the difference between an American- and a European- (usually German-) bred dog. The biggest difference is that AKC-registered dogs have more sloping backs and

more extreme angulation of the hind legs. They also tend to be larger overall with a more refined head. By contrast, the European German Shepherd (SV-reistered) tends to have a more rounded ('roached') back.

SV stands for *Verein fuer Deutsche Schaeferhunde* which is the German club for German Shepherds and

the largest breed club in the world. One advantage of European (SV-registered) dogs is that German Shepherds from Germany are only approved for breeding if they have passed a long string of tests, so much of your homework is done for you.

The difference in conformation is only really important if you want to show your dog, because winners in SV shows will not necessarily also win in AKC shows and vice versa.

So, what about Alsatians?

If you are confused about the distinction between an Alsatian and a German Shepherd, you will be pleased to discover it is only in name. The breed was officially known as the Alsatian in Britain from after the First World War until 1977 when its name was changed back to German Shepherd.

4. FINDING THE LITTER

DECIDING WHAT YOU'RE LOOKING FOR

Before you actually go in search of new litters, you might want to sort out some preferences in your own mind. What do you want your German Shepherd for? Do you prefer a medium or longer coat? Do you have a strong colour preference? Would you prefer a girl or a boy?

Unless you live alone, make sure you involve all members of the family and household in these decisions from the start. The more say they've had in choosing your dog, the more likely they'll be to actively engage with and care for him, and the less likely they'll be to shirk their dog-walking, poo-picking responsibilities.

Are you looking for a pet? Or something more?

Do you have specific expectations of your Shepherd: show dog, herder or disability assistant for example? If you do, will need to do in-depth research into the temperaments and abilities of the parents.

As far as the quality of the puppy is concerned, an experienced breeder will usually rate the puppies as 'pet', 'competition' or 'breeding'.

Pet quality doesn't mean the puppies are flawed in temperament or health – those are never desirable. It just means they wouldn't do well in show classes because of a fault, and that fault might be as simple as its colouring for example.

Competition quality means they should be acceptable for the show ring, because they have no disqualifying features.

Breeding quality dogs are extremely difficult to identify at the puppy stage, even when they are from the very-highest-quality backgrounds. If you're serious about going into breeding you'd be better off looking for an adult dog you can assess more accurately.

Coat type

German Shepherds' coats can be medium or long, but they almost all have a double coat: a dense undercoat of short hairs which protect them from extreme temperatures (both hot and cold), and a top coat of longer, straighter 'guard' hairs which repel moisture and dirt. The denser the undercoat, the fluffier the dog will be and the more grooming it will need.

Medium: According to the breed standards, a good German Shepherd has a double coat of 'medium' length. (This is sometimes referred to as 'variety a').

Long: Long-coated German Shepherds (sometimes referred to as 'variety b') are considered faulty by most showing standards, although they are now officially recognised by the breed standard in the UK. If you are wanting to compete in showing classes, then check the standards in your country before choosing a long-haired German Shepherd.

Lots of people prefer the way these dogs look so many breeders breed them specially. They can be born to short-coated parents but the gene is recessive so the longer coats are rarer.

The longer coats can also be difficult to pick out at an early age, but they are usually noticeable by nine or ten weeks.

Colour

Deciding on the colouring of your dog can also narrow your search. If it's important to you for your dog to be close to the breeding standard then choose one with 'rich' colouring – typically tan or red with a black saddle, or entirely black.

White German Shepherds: While these aren't uncommon and many people prefer them, they are considered faulty by the breed standard, even though their colouring is not associated with health defects or shown to be detrimental to their ability as working dogs.

They often lack the double coat and, through generations of breed separation, have also developed slightly differently in conformation and movement. As a result, in 1999 they became recognised as an independent breed by the United Kennel Club.

Shape

There is disagreement among Kennel Clubs about the soundness of the show-strain of the breed. Essentially, many German Shepherds bred for showing have an accentuated sloping back, a trait that is often the cause of poor gait in the hind legs. Needless to say, working-pedigree lines, like those used as service dogs, usually have the more traditional straight back of the breed.

Girl or boy?

Honestly, that's up to you. Unless you're wanting to breed with your dog someday, I don't believe there's much in it.

Males are larger in both height and weight – weighing between 75 and 95 pounds (34-43kg). They have larger heads and heavier bone and can be prouder, braver and more territorial. They can also be more affectionate and dependent. On the downside, males don't always get on well with other males and, if un-neutered, can go in search of females and lift their legs indoors to mark their territory.

Females are usually smaller and lighter – weighing between 60 and 70 pounds (27-32kg). They tend to fight less, but when they do they are more ferocious. Many say they are more intelligent and make better guard dogs. On the downside, if a female is un-neutered she will come into heat two to three times a year for three weeks at a time.

Neutering really is the answer for both sexes and there is more on this in the chapter 'Going forward'.

TIMING

As well as getting an idea of the sort of puppy you're looking for, you'll need to figure out approximately how long the process will take, and then decide on the best time to bring a puppy into your life and home.

Starting the search

If you decide on a pet-quality Shepherd, your search should take no more than a few months.

However, if you're looking for a dog that is competition- or breeding-quality you can expect to be looking for up to two years before actually bringing your puppy home. If this is the case, it is likely you'll be in contact with a breeder before the litter is born, or even before the mother is mated, which would give you the possibility of meeting her and assessing her temperament when she is not feeling overprotective of her young.

Whatever your decision, you should also start investigating the best route to finding puppies for sale, ideally in your area. This might be a kennel club, a publication, a website or several of each. (There is more on this in the next section: 'Buy responsibly').

Adverts often feature males available for breeding, so if you see a male you particularly like you could ask the owner to keep you informed of new litters he has fathered.

Browsing around will give you a sense of what the puppies look like when they are newborn and very young, and also of when puppies are advertised –

some people advertise their litters very early, and some only when the puppies are almost ready to go to their new homes.

The best time to pick up your puppy

German Shepherds are pack animals and don't like being alone, so this should be at the beginning of a stretch when most of the family will be home and able to care for the puppy full-time for most – if not all – of the day. If you are retired this mightn't be a consideration, but if you are a working family with school-going children, for example, you should aim to pick your puppy up early in the school holidays.

The weather is another consideration. If you live in a country where the summer and winter temperatures are very different, or the wet seasons are extreme, then getting your puppy at the start of a warm or dry season will make for much easier exercising and toilet training.

Luckily most breeders are likely to have taken these factors into consideration, and you will find that the most puppies are available at the start of summer and the long school holidays.

Generally, good breeders will also not let their puppies go to their new homes before they are eight or nine weeks old. Ideally you want to visit the litter and meet the puppies around the six-week mark, if not before. The next step then is to decide on the best time to bring your puppy home. Work out eight weeks before your ideal date, and – unless you are already waiting for a specific female to have her puppies – that is when you can start looking out for brand new litters.

BUYING RESPONSIBLY

You might know someone who has German Shepherd puppies ready for their permanent homes, and they might be the nicest people on earth, but that doesn't necessarily make them good or responsible breeders. German Shepherd breeders range from excellent, to acceptable, to people who shouldn't be allowed to keep dogs at all, never mind use them for breeding. So, whether you're relying on word-of-mouth, advertisements on the internet, or in magazine and newspapers, when you start looking for your puppy, discretion is key.

Good places to look for reputable breeders:
- The websites of Kennel Clubs and German Shepherd Dog (GSD) clubs
- Dog shows.

Good people to ask:
- GSD club members
- Breeders at dog shows
- Dog trainers
- Dog behaviour experts
- Vets
- Groomers
- Boarding kennel personnel.

Reading the adverts

If you're looking at adverts, be sure to read between the lines. Don't look for a bargain – good German Shepherds aren't cheap. And be equally wary of puppies priced well over the average – silly money is unlikely to guarantee you a miracle dog. But most importantly of all, watch out for puppy dealers. Also referred to as puppy farmers, these are people who breed puppies in substandard conditions, but sell them from normal-looking homes which are, in reality, nothing more than a shop front.

You want to be sure you're buying a healthy, happy puppy and at the same time not unknowingly supporting the cruel puppy trade. So when arranging to see a litter, make sure it's with a responsible breeder. This is easier said than done because puppy farmers and dealers can be tricky to identify, but these are some of the tell-tale signs that should make you think twice about an advert.

- Puppy farmers often use the same contact number on more than one advert. If the advert is posted on the internet, do a search on the number to see if it has been used on any other puppy adverts.
- They often use the same descriptions, word-for-word, in more than one advert. Search a key phrase in the wording to locate duplicate advertising.
- Photos of the puppies may also have been used on other adverts. Right click on the photo, then select 'search Google for image' to find out.
- A vet will not vaccinate a puppy before four weeks of age so if a person is advertising a vaccinated puppy that is three weeks old, stay away.
- Don't be fooled by promises of 'free puppy packs'. These don't necessarily make the sellers any more legitimate.
- If the breeder claims to be Kennel Club registered, check this with the Kennel Club.
- An inexperienced breeder might use the word 'thoroughbred' instead of 'purebred'.

De-coding the adverts

Ads for German Shepherds are often decorated with seemingly undecipherable letter 'codes'. Most of these relate to accreditation of conformation, obedience or suitability for breeding, and are beyond the need-to-know parameters of this book, but the following examples are worth noting because they relate to the dogs' health:

- 'a' normal: a German certification relating to the hips
- KKL-I, KKL-II: indicates recommended for breeding, with 'I' being better than 'II'. (A dog with these letters will have passed all necessary health checks.)

- OFA: Orthopaedic Foundation for Animals rating (usually for hip or elbow dysplasia)
- vWD normal: rating of test for von Willebrand's disease (a bleeding disorder).

The call

When you're happy with the advert, it's time to make contact. You can do this by email to start with, and many people are more comfortable with email, but you will learn much more by speaking to the breeder in person. These are some key questions to ask:

- Did you breed the puppies yourself?
  - *It's imperative that they did, so you can meet the mother.*

- Are the puppies currently in the place where they were bred?
  - *That is where you need to see the litter.*
- How many puppies are, or were there, in the litter?
  - *It's always best to see the puppies together. Avoid seeing just one.*
- Have the puppies had any health problems? And have the mother or father had any health problems, in particular elbow dysplasia, hip dysplasia or Von Willebrand disease?
  - *If they undermine the importance of health concerns with the breed, such as hip and elbow ratings, simply because their dogs reportedly haven't shown signs of them, take it as an indication of an inexperienced breeder.*
- Is this the mother's first litter?
  - *You want to find out how many litters she has had because a German Shepherd bitch should have no more than three to four litters in her lifetime, and these should be no closer together than once a year. A breeder who doesn't respect this is putting money above the wellbeing of the dog and shouldn't be encouraged.*
- Is it only German Shepherds that you breed?
  - *Multi-breed breeders are often backyard breeders or puppy farmers.*
- Have the puppies been treated for worms?
  - *Ideally the puppies will have had at least one deworming treatment before going to their new homes.*
- Have they been given their first vaccinations?
  - *Vaccination requirements vary from country to country, but initial vaccinations generally comprise*

two doses with an interval of two to four weeks. The first of these is usually given before eight weeks of age, but not before three to four weeks.

- Have they been microchipped?
  - *This is a tiny chip injected under your puppy's skin at the back of his neck. It holds his unique number which links to your contact details and, unlike a collar and tag, it stays there for life. If they have been microchipped that's a bonus, but it's not essential. See 'Visit the vet' in the chapter 'The first week'.*
- Does the breeder have the relevant paperwork?
  - *genuine registration and pedigree documents where applicable,*
  - *extensive health certifications and ratings,*
  - *proof of any showing, working or obedience competition achievements by the litter's parents and relatives,*
  - *a record of vaccinations and deworming treatments (this will need to be seen by your vet at your puppy's first visit, as well as taken to any training classes or boarding kennels),*
  - *the details of the puppy's microchipping (if relevant) so you can change the contact details to your own.*

A good and responsible breeder:
- will be happy to answer all your questions on the phone.
- will ask questions of you too, to make sure their puppies are going to excellent homes.
- will be able to compare the parent dogs to the German Shepherd standard.
  - *If they don't know about the German Shepherd standard, or belittle it, you should stay away.*

- will have photos and possibly video clips of the puppies' parents and relatives, and be happy to send you more by phone or email if you feel you need them (especially if a visit means a lengthy journey on your part).
- will give you the impression of actively loving and nurturing each pup, as well as the mother, to make sure they are well socialised.
- will be happy to arrange a time for you to visit the puppies and their mother in the place where they were born and raised.
- will be happy for you to have more than one visit before pick up if you feel you need it.
- might offer to take the dog back if you can't keep it. Some breeders even include a contract requiring you to contact them first if you ever need to give the dog up.

Never get a puppy if
you have any doubts
about the seller or breeder.

A responsible breeder will NEVER:
- offer to deliver the puppy to you.
- offer to meet you at a random place.
- tell you the mother is out at the vets, or for any other reason. If she isn't there, the puppy most likely wasn't bred there, or there could be a problem with her.
- suggest that you breed your puppy for money. (Good breeders breed their German Shepherds for love, and seldom make money from their efforts.)
- push you for payment.

Once you've found a litter of puppies you like the look and sound of, and you're sure they're healthy, happy and from a good home environment, set up your visit or visits.

Then find or buy a soft, comfortable blanket to take with you. This is so that, if you do reserve a puppy, you can leave it with him until you pick him up. It will absorb the smells of his mother and litter mates until then, and, help to make the separation less stressful.

Then the countdown begins …

5. TIME TO CHOOSE

When the day arrives you'll be eager to get going, but before you set off, remember to take that soft, comfy blanket.

WHICH PUPPY?

With some dog breeds, every puppy in a litter is distinctly different from the next, but with a litter of German Shepherd pups you're likely to be greeted by a writhing bundle of dark furry gorgeousness. Certainly at first.

If the puppies' coats are almost all black, they will probably become black and gold as they mature, but it's near impossible to predict the colouring of the adult dog at this stage.

There's also not much indication of coat length until the puppies are around ten weeks - especially as the pups of medium-coated Shepherds can turn out to be long-coated.

So, what now?

You've seen pictures of the parents, and possibly even the grandparents and other relatives. Looks-wise that is the best indicator of how the puppies will turn out, and presumably you're already happy with that. What you'll be scrutinising are temperament and health.

But not yet. You'll be itching to spend time with the puppies, but wait until you're satisfied with these other basic checks.

The environment and breeder

Look for signs of where the puppies are being raised. Are you as sure as you can be that this is where they've grown up? If you suspect their usual base is somewhere out of sight, or off the premises, then you need to be super cautious.

Try to make sense of the puppies' immediate environment too. Is it warm, friendly and homely? Are they being brought up in clean conditions?

And watch how the breeder interacts with them. Is it genuinely loving and understanding of each puppy's individual nature?

Ideally, the litter is being brought up right underfoot where the puppies can benefit from lots of human contact. A litter that is growing up in the kitchen area of a family home with several animal-loving children, for example, is likely to have a far better start than one raised in the back room of a quiet one-person home. Puppies that haven't had enough positive human interaction from six weeks of age until the time they go to their new homes can have personality issues for the rest of their lives. Because this time is out of your hands, don't underestimate the importance of this check.

The mother

It's well worth spending some time with the mother too, and any other relatives if possible, for an idea of temperament. They must be friendly and good-natured if that is what you hope for in your puppy.

It's also important that they are healthy, happy and

confident – not shy, slinking away, or aggressive towards you. That said, you might need to make allowances for the mother if she is a little protective of her pups.

The paperwork

All paperwork can be subject to faking; nothing can guarantee how your dog will turn out. And anyway there's no reason your German Shepherd shouldn't be a wonderful companion without any paperwork at all. But why not minimise the risk? If you were promised any paperwork on collection, you should ask to see it now.

Registration papers – these are the certificates – either for the whole litter or the individual puppy – that record your dog's registration number. They are issued by reputable registries like your national kennel club, and dogs imported from Germany are usually registered with the SV (the German Shepherd Club in Germany). Beware of smaller, lesser-known registries as they will sometimes register dogs without the proper checks. These documents also serve as proof of your dog's pure ancestry, because to be registered with a legitimate registry, your dog must first have a pedigree.

Pedigree – this is your dog's family tree and lists the breeding decisions that have been made. It is less official than the registration papers because a dog that is registered is always a pedigree, but a pedigree dog is not necessarily registered.

Health certificates – Check any health clearance certificates, in particular for hip and elbow dysplasia. Many breeders supply a guarantee with their pups that covers them against it. Health clearance is especially important if you are considering breeding with your dog going forward, because any health issues could bar his or her progeny from being registered.

Vaccination certificates – you should also see these if you were told about them on the phone.

The puppies

Finally, we get to the puppies, but still try not to let your heart rule your head. Not entirely. Not yet. Study their behaviour and make sure they are:

- confident, not shy,
- friendly, and not hostile,
- interested in you and everything around them, and
- energetic.

And make sure they appear healthy. They should not have any of these:

- missing hair
- fleas or ticks
- crusted skin
- discharge from the eyes, ears or nose
- soiling from faeces
- irritation around the bottom
- diarrhoea
- vomiting
- coughs and sneezes
- dehydration (test by pulling a fold of skin and releasing. It should bounce back into place.)
- pale gums.

Which puppy?

All going well, you can finally take your pick. But which one? These are some tips that could help you with your decision:

- If you are absolutely sure you want a girl, you

could ask the breeder to remove the boys while you meet the girls, or vice versa.

- Don't rush this. Sit down with the puppies and spend all the time you need with them. Watch them playing, and, see how they interact with you and their litter mates.
- Ask the breeder for their opinion, because they will have experience with the breed and have had time to get to know the individual pups.

- Some people place the puppies on their backs as a test of temperament. Ideally they want their pick of the litter to struggle against them for a few seconds

and then submit and let them hold him in place.
- You could also try the 'follow test', judging the pups on the ones that follow you.
- It's often said that you don't choose your dog or puppy, it chooses you, and many people vouch for this. One puppy might spend your entire visit convincing you he's the one you want to take home. If that happens, he probably is.

More basic checks

Now examine your chosen puppy more thoroughly.
- Whichever pup you choose, it should be happy, healthy, interactive, confident and curious.
- Check its teeth. Its upper and lower teeth should be in line, with the upper front teeth just forward over the lower front teeth.
- There must be no sign of mucus from the nose, bottom or genitals.
- The ears should be clean and not smelly.

When you've settled on your choice, you should feel convinced you've chosen the best dog in the world and wonder how on earth you got so lucky.

Before you leave

Money – In all likelihood, the breeder will ask for a deposit to secure your puppy. Make sure you get a receipt and a written agreement that the contract is only binding on condition that the puppy is in good health when you collect it.

If there is no litter registration number as yet, the breeder should give you a signed bill of sale that includes:
- reassurance that the number will be available by the time of sale

- details of the puppy's breed, sex, colour and date of birth
- the registered names of your puppy's parents (sire and dam), ideally with their registration numbers.

Food and care – Find out whatever you can about meals. What are the puppies being fed at the moment? How much and how often? Ask to see the food so you can source it now and be sure of giving him exactly what he is used to when you bring him home.

The extra mile – Finally ask the breeder if you can leave your soft blanket with the litter so that when you pick him up, you will be able to bring all those familiar mother-puppy smells with him into his new home.

6. PREPARING FOR THE BIG DAY

It almost goes without saying that when you pick up your bundle of joy, and destruction too, yes, you will need buckets of love, oodles of patience and a fantastic sense of humour. But before then you will also need to do a surprising amount of planning, puppy-proofing and purchasing of paraphernalia ...

Things to do

- Arrange a date to pick up your puppy – not before he is eight weeks' old. If you are travelling by car, it should be a day when at least one other person can accompany the driver.
- Book a visit to the vet for about two days after pick-up.
- If you have other dogs, make sure their vaccinations are up to date.
- Puppy proof your home:
  - Secure the property. This is the most important thing you can do to keep your dog safe. If you have a garden or yard, ensure the borders are escape proof. Totally! German Shepherds are gifted diggers, jumpers and climbers.
  - If there is a pool, pond or any form of deep or dangerous water he could fall into, fence it off.
  - Check that there are no chemicals within reach (pesticides, weed killers, fertilisers, etc).

- Cover or hide electricity cables and wires.
- Secure any unstable furniture such as bookcases that could come crashing down.
- Remove sharp objects and small things he could choke on.
- Remove valuables from the floor.
- Apply citronella or anti-chew to everything of great value that will be within his reach.
- **Plants** – Some plants in your house and garden may be harmful if your puppy ingests them, especially in volume. There's no need to go digging up your entire garden, but it's worth identifying the more dangerous varieties now so you can move them if necessary, or at least keep an informed eye on your puppy's grazing. It would be well worth checking online for a comprehensive list and doing an inspection of your own plants, but in the meanwhile here are ten common plants that top the red-alert list:

  Tomatoes, Potatoes, Crocuses, Lilies, Tulips, Nandina, Foxtails, Sago Palms (ornamental house plants), Castor Beans and Azaleas.

  Other common varieties to keep an eye out for include:

  Aloe Vera, Asparagus Fern, Corn Cockle, Cyclamen, Daffodil, Holly Berry, Foxglove, Ivy, Jade, Jerusalem Cherry, Jessamine, Hyacinth, Milkweed, Mistletoe, Oleander, Rhododendron and Water Hemlock.

- Decide on his special place, a suitable comfy space that he can make his own. Assuming he will be allowed inside the house, this is where his crate will be positioned if you choose to use one, or simply his basket and toys. Either way this special place should be somewhere central – somewhere he can feel safe, but without feeling isolated or excluded. An ideal position would be against a wall in the room that most of you spend the most time in during the day.

Things to buy, make or borrow

- **Soft blanket** – you might already have left this with the litter when you chose your puppy.
- **Crate** (also commonly referred to as a **cage, den or puppy pen**) – this is optional of course, but it would serve as your puppy's own space, a special place where he can be safe, quiet and keep his toys. There is more about this in the next three chapters, but for now choose one that is at least big enough for your puppy's basket or bed, toys and bowls – and for a full-grown German Shepherd to stand up, turn around and lie down in. Wire cages are better ventilated than plastic ones, offer better views, and are easily collapsible for storage or transport.
- **Comfortable bed** – this could be a basket or a dog cushion, the mattress from a baby crib or even a folded blanket, as long as it is soft, comfortable and washable.
- **Collar** – choose one that is soft, lightweight and comfortable. He will soon outgrow it and you can choose a sturdier one then if that's what you prefer.
- **Dog tag** – no need for cow bells. Choose one that is small and light and have it engraved with his name and your contact details.
- **Harness** – harnesses offer little control over an

adult German Shepherd but it's a good idea to have one of these for your puppy because they put no pressure on his throat when he is learning to walk on the lead. This should be a suitable size, adjustable, and comfortable.

- **Short lead** (up to six feet long) – again, nice and light. He's only little.

- **Extendable lead** – this can make walks more enjoyable for you and your puppy. But it should be used carefully and only once he is used to the short lead. The freedom these leads allow makes them a risk for your puppy, people and/or other animals and, as a result, they are not always permitted in parks and conservation areas.

- **Bowls** – go for a non-tip, non-slip design. Also consider a non-spill travel bowl for car trips, and a crate bowl that clips onto the door or side of your puppy's crate so that it can't be overturned. Remember your puppy will be a large dog before long, so consider whether to invest in big bowls or get small bowls for now and upsize in time. If the food will be kept outside, you might want to look at ant-resistant bowls. The alternative is to put his food bowl inside a shallow, wider bowl or plate filled with water.

- **Food** – start with the food your puppy has been given at his breeders. After that you can move him on to the brand of your choice. If you are concerned about making the best decision, consult your vet at his first check-up.

- **Treats** – you will need lots of these. They are fantastic motivators when your puppy is first learning the rules, and just as good for reinforcing good behaviour. Choose treats that are suitable for puppies and avoid too many additives and preservatives, including sugar and salt. As a rough guide, the fewer ingredients the better.

- **Treat pouch** – a handy pocket for loose treats that keeps your own pockets from constantly smelling of dog food.

- **Chews** – your puppy will spend around four hours of each day munching on things, so it's up to you to provide what you want him to do his chewing on. Chews make a fabulous alternative to table legs and leather shoes, but with a young puppy avoid any chews that can splinter. Antler horns are good, and so are hollow chew toys filled with treats.

- **Toys** – he will need plenty of these in all shapes, sizes, textures, colours and smells – toys that roll, bounce, squeak and light up. He will chew on them, play with them and even snuggle up with them for hours. It's quite possible that he'll favour an old sock over an expensive toy, but can a puppy have too many toys? I think not. (It's wise to avoid giving him old shoes because, smart as he is, he's unlikely to differentiate between old and new when he slips inside your shoe closet.)

- **Anti-chew or citronella** – it's worth investing in either of these to spray onto those things he absolutely must not chew on. Expensive chair legs for example.

- **Poop scoop bags** – choose biodegradable to do your bit for the environment.

- **Wee mats/newspaper**

- **Carpet cleaner** – pet friendly

- **Odour eliminator** – pet friendly
- **Hot water bottle** – strong and covered
- **Grooming brush or glove** – suited to his coat type
- **Dog seatbelt, pet carrier or dog guard** – if he is likely to travel by car.

Indoor extras

- **Baby gates/stair gates** – these are far better than closed doors for keeping a room off-limits. But stay away from stretch gates that he could get his head stuck in.
- **Exercise pen** – this is useful if you are leaving him for a couple of hours because it is big enough (usually about four feet by four feet) for him to sleep, play and poop in if necessary.

Outdoor extras

- **Kennel** – if your puppy's likely to spend a lot of time outside when he's older, consider building or buying a doghouse. There's a vast range of luxury kennels on the market for you to choose from or replicate, but make sure the floor is raised.
- Other useful features are:
  ◦ removable side for cleaning (often the floor or door)
  ◦ doorway that keeps wind and rain out of the sleeping area. (This could be a hanging rubber dog-flap, a patio space or overhang, or even a double doorway.)
- **Kennel bedding** – any kennel will need its own soft bedding.
- **Outdoor water bowl** – large and tip-proof

- **Paddling pool** – if you live in a warm climate or have hot summers, a children's paddling pool is great fun and a fabulous cooler.

Setting the rules

Before you bring your newest family member into your home, it's essential for you and the other members of the household to have a serious chat about the rules.

Decide among yourselves where your puppy will be allowed, and when. Make sure you are all in agreement about which rooms and pieces of furniture are off-limit. And make sure everyone understands that sneaking him into an off-limit area, or letting him break the rules in any other way, would just be unfair and confusing for your puppy in the long run.

If your family agrees, quite sensibly, that your puppy's not to be allowed on your best furniture, it doesn't mean you need to treat him like an underling. You can compromise by making sure he has a place he can call his own – a special cushion placed next to the forbidden chair for example.

Choosing a name

Whether you choose this now or wait until he's home, his name is more important than you might think. You will be using it many times a day for years to come so it must be something he will easily recognise.

- Animals respond better to shorter names – one-syllable names with a hard consonant or consonants like Duke or Zac for example, or two-syllable names such as Pop-py, Os-car or Til-ly. You might love the name Penelope or Ophelia, but your dog would thank you for calling it Pen or Oophy instead.
- Make sure the name you choose doesn't sound too much like a commonly used command: No, Sit, Down, Stay, Come, Here, Good or Fetch. Beau and Jo, for example, sound too much like No.
- And don't choose a name that sounds like that of another member of the household. If your mother is called Anne, don't call puppy Dan; if your cat is Tigger, don't call puppy Digger or Trigger.

- Choose a name that is easy to call out. 'M' and 'n' sounds are soft which makes them more difficult to call out loud than harder consonants like 'p', 't' and 'z'. Molly, say, is a less effective pet name than Pippy.
- Never give any dog a name you wouldn't be happy calling out loud in public, but for a German Shepherd specifically, choose one that reflects the strength and majesty of the breed.

7. PICKING UP YOUR PUPPY

'Happiness is a warm puppy'
Charles M Schulz

The big day has finally arrived. If possible, pick him up early in the day so he can spend lots of time in his new environment before facing his first night without his mother and litter mates.

Remember, if you are driving, to make sure someone is with you to comfort and hold him.

Before you go
- If you haven't already set up his special place in a safe but central spot, do that now. Crate or no crate, furnish it with the comfortable dog basket or bed, some toys, and also some treats if you like.
- And if you haven't already sprayed your most valued furniture with anti-chew, now's a very good time.

Things to take
- The remainder of the payment (if necessary)
- An absorbent mat (or similar protection) in case he relieves himself in the car
- Poo bags and cleaning cloths
- Two bowls (one for food and one for water)
- A small amount of food (in a container)

- A bottle of water
- A small selection of toys and chews
- A backup soft blanket or cushion is also a good idea (in case something has happened to the one you left with the breeder)
- A collar or harness and your lead (not extendable).

The big moment

There at last and this is it! Give your new family member and best friend a gargantuan cuddle, have a play and check that he's still in good health:

- happy, confident and curious,
- that there are no signs of mucus from the nose, bottom or genitals,
- and that his ears are clean and not smelly.

In the excitement

Apart from your new and perfect puppy, don't forget to come away with:

- the blanket you left, if you left one
- the registration papers
- any other relevant paperwork including:
  - a receipt of payment,
  - vaccination certificate,
  - microchip number and provider details (so you can register your puppy under your name and with its new address and contact details).

It's also worth double checking his food type (just in case it's been changed), and finding out what times he has been having his meals.

And last but definitely not least, remember to thank the mother as well as the breeder for your beautiful puppy.

Travelling

Make sure your puppy is feeling safe and happy to be with you before you take him away for good. He is totally reliant on you now, so put yourself into those little paws that are being taken away from their mother and litter mates. Realise that he is leaving the only place he has ever known and, if you're driving, getting into a car for the first time too! Ask yourself, "How would I be feeling now?" and "What would I need from this new person or family?" You'd want to feel safe and secure, loved and cherished.

It's advisable to put on his collar or harness before you set off. This is best done with two people so one of you can hold and distract him while the other puts it on. If you're using a collar, you don't want it too tight or too loose. You should just be able to put two fingers between the collar and the puppy's neck. If you've brought a harness, you should also be able to fit two fingers (and no more) between your puppy and the harness at any point.

If you're travelling by car, the puppy would be happiest being held by the passenger in the back seat. He would need to be held securely, so that the driver is not distracted, and be given love and constant reassurance on the journey. However, where you put him in the car will depend on the laws in your country, as holding him in the back seat could affect your insurance.

Your puppy will probably be too anxious for toys, but offer them anyway.

If the journey home is a long one, you'll need to attach the lead to his collar and stop every hour – more if you can. Like people, dogs can suffer from travel sickness, so it is possible he might be feeling a little ill or even be sick on the journey. He will also need these breaks for a walk and the chance to go to the toilet, but always keep him on the lead. Though he's unlikely to stray from you, this would be a terrible place for him to get loose.

At every break, offer him some of the food and water in the bowls you've brought along.

8. THE HOMECOMING

Give him a chance to wee before going inside.

Carry him into the house and put him near or in his special place, or his crate, with the door wide open. Sit beside him, arrange the blanket smelling of his mother and litter mates in his basket, and give him a treat.

Then let him explore his special place and the house, always staying by his side. Let him venture into **all** the areas he will be allowed to roam, so that he knows this is home. If there are areas of the house that will be off limits to him, then it is better not to let him in there from the start than to change the rules at some later stage.

Even if you intend for your puppy to be an outdoors dog, he should have access to at least one room at this stage, because he is not yet ready to be left outside on his own.

All the treats today should be given in his crate or special area – his very own bedroom. His comfy blanket should stay there and it is advisable to feed him there too. Do everything you can think of to make him feel that **this** is the best and safest place in the world. If there is a crate and the design is very open, cover it with a blanket leaving gaps he can see out of.

Puppies wee about once an hour and poop several times a day, so take him outside every hour if you can.

He will still piddle and poop in the house because he is so little, can't talk to you, and has no idea that doing this inside is a no-no. Toilet training is covered in more detail later on, but for now be sure to clean up after him very well, and use an odour eliminator.

Your puppy needs 18-22 hours' sleep a day at this age, and today he is likely to need even more than that. But your presence is essential for his peace of mind so, when you are sitting quietly, let him sit with you and sleep on your lap or close by.

Make sure there is always fresh water available to him, and that he knows where it is. Feed him what he is used to and, as far as practical, at the times he is used to. At this age he is most probably on four evenly-spaced meals a day. Aim to give him his last meal of the day a good two hours before his bedtime, so he has a chance to go to the toilet before settling down for his first night.

9. THE FIRST NIGHT

Crunch time! He had his supper a couple of hours ago and it's time for bed.

- Take him outside for a last chance to go to the toilet. Stay with him in the place you'd most like him to go, and, be patient.
- Back inside, make sure his crate or safe space is as appealing as possible, with his comfortable bed and his soft blanket. (In the short term, some people make this space in their own bedrooms, setting it up by the side of their beds. Considering the trauma of this first night, to your puppy and yourselves, there is a lot to be said for this. He still wouldn't be able to snuggle up the way he's used to, but at least he could see you and hear you and know he's not alone.)

If his sleeping place is a metal crate, the openness still leaves your puppy quite exposed. So if you've chosen the crate option and haven't already done so, put a blanket over all or part of it, making sure he can always see out.

It's a good idea to make a warm, but not too warm, hot water bottle, and wrap it carefully into his comfy blanket. This is to replicate the body warmth of his mother and litter mates when they're snuggled up. Some people also put a ticking clock in the bed to mimic a heartbeat. And if the special place is not in your room, you could leave a radio playing softly to give him the sense he is not alone.

Scatter some toys and treats and
make sure he has access to some clean water in his non-
tip or clip-on bowl.

If the space is big enough for a place to relieve
himself – aside from the bedding and bowls, then cover
this with newspaper or an absorbent wee mat.

When crunch time comes, don't fuss over him. Just
put him in his crate or special place with a treat, as
though he's the luckiest puppy in the world, and close
the door: be it a cage door, room door or baby gate.

In all likelihood he will cry at first, but he'll be
warm, comfortable, fed and tired, so it shouldn't be for
long.

Don't give him attention when he cries, because
then he'll just keep on crying. If you do want to tell him
he's a good dog, then wait until he's settled.

What about toilet time? If he is in your room, and
you hear him shuffling around in the night, get up and
take him outside. He won't want to wee in his crate or
sleeping place if he can help it. (And it won't be long
before he doesn't need this break at all.)

If he's not in your room, you'll need to set an
alarm for the middle of the night so you can get up and
take him outside. Alternatively, and only if you've laid
down a wee mat, you could wait until very early the
next morning. You'll need to do that for the next few
weeks at least.

10. NEW PUPPY SAFETY

People

The best way to keep your puppy safe is through your and your family's and housemates' own diligence.

- Be careful to keep doors closed and open where necessary, and don't shut them too quickly – your new 'shadow' could be right on your heels.
- Don't let your puppy play around cars or tackle the lawn mower.
- Don't leave dangerous objects or poisonous substances in his reach.
- Don't feed him or let him get hold of 'people food', and especially not chocolate!
- Don't let him near the edges of deep water, or high places: balconies, low window ledges, or unsecured staircases.
- Be careful with rocking or reclining chairs.
- Keep electrical cords well out of reach – apart from shock there is the danger of something falling on him (a heavy iron or boiling kettle for example).

If you want to be really proactive, put yourself in his paws for a moment. Being super careful not to underestimate his strength, speed or intelligence, get down on all fours and see what temptations call. Then take these away. Puppy-proof your home and make it as difficult as you can for him to get into any form of trouble.

Then supervise him, just as you would a busy toddler.

Small children

If you have small children, it is very important to supervise them when they are playing with your puppy. There is more on the subject later in the book, when your puppy will have become more boisterous, but small children must understand NOW that your puppy is NOT a toy.

- They must not be allowed to pick him up without adult supervision.
- They must not be allowed to disturb him if he is sleeping or has taken himself to a quiet place.
- They must not run around squealing, and if the puppy becomes over-excited they must calm down and keep still.
- They should be allowed to play calm games, but nothing involving wrestling or tugging.
- They should always stay on their feet while playing with the puppy. If children writhe on the ground with your puppy, he will treat them like his litter mates and mouth and bite.

Your other dogs (if you have them)

- Keep introductions short and sweet to start with, with your puppy on a lead to stop him from getting too close.
- If possible, let them meet for the first time away from home. Ideally, choose somewhere your older dog has not been before so that the excitement of the new environment will dilute the puppy's presence. Try to ensure the meeting place is somewhere no other dogs are likely to go (as your

puppy will not be not protected by his vaccinations yet).

- Stand still or walk slowly when you let your puppy and your older dog meet, and try not to interfere.
- When you get home, if you have a garden, let the dogs meet there again in the same way before going inside. Let your puppy into the house first, before letting the older dog in.
- Lift any existing dog toys and food bowls off the floor for a few days.
- If you are worried about your puppy's safety, use a baby gate or stair gate to separate the dogs in the short term, or put the puppy in his crate or a pen while the dogs get used to each other.
- Make sure all members of the family give the older dog more attention than usual.

Multiple dogs

If you already have more than one other dog, the process is the same, but you should introduce the puppy to one dog at a time.

Cats

When your puppy is this young, he is unlikely to be a problem for your cat. Besides, German Shepherds generally get on well with the family cat, especially if they have grown up with it. But, to be on the safe side, care should always be taken when he meets any other small pets or animals.

- Keep him on a lead when they first meet, and have a lovely puppy treat at the ready. If your cat responds by hissing and spitting to begin with, your puppy will most likely retreat. But if the cat

runs away, be ready to
distract the puppy with the treat so he doesn't
give chase.

- Always restrain him around the cat until he learns
  the cat is not something to be chased.
- And distract him with a toy or a game to teach him
  that playing with people is more fun than chasing
  the cat. Okay so it's debatable, but that's what we
  want him to think.
- If you need to keep your puppy and the cat
  separated while you are out, use the puppy pen or
  a stair gate.
- Make sure the cat has safe places high up that it can
  reach instead of having to run away.

11. DANGER ALERT!

Non-edibles

Your puppy will be chewing everything now, it's what puppies do best – either because they are teething or because they are using their mouths to find out about the world around them. But there are some non-edibles it's particularly important to keep out of reach:

- Medication – human medication is the biggest cause of pet poisoning.
- Anti-freeze and other chemicals – many of these are sweet-tasting.
- Paint thinner
- Toothpaste
- Sponges
- Pesticides
- Household cleaners (including toilet cleaners)
- A surprisingly high number of household and garden plants can be poisonous when eaten in large amounts. (See the shortlist and advice in 'Preparing for the big day'.)
- Small metal objects like coins, and nuts and bolts
- Pins, needles and other sharp objects.

Edibles that are poisonous for dogs

It's always best to feed your puppy or dog actual puppy or dog food, and simply stay clear of treats from your own plate. But there are some foods that you must never let him get hold of never mind feed him because, while they are perfectly safe for human consumption, they are potentially fatal to dogs. These include:

- Chocolate (especially dark chocolate)
- Xylitol (artificial sweetener, commonly used in sweets and gum, but also in some sweet foods like low-calorie cake)
- Alcohol
- Onion
- Garlic
- Grapes or raisins
- Avocado

Also keep dogs away from

- Soft bones (especially from chicken or pork, as they can get stuck in your dog's throat)
- Macadamia nuts
- Fruit pips or seeds
- Potato peels or green potatoes
- Rhubarb leaves
- Baker's yeast or yeast dough
- Broccoli
- Caffeine
- Mushrooms
- Persimmons
- Hops (generally in beer)

This is just a shortlist of some of the more common non-edibles and household foods you should keep away from your dog. It's not absolute so it's worth keeping an eye out for fuller and newly published lists.

Swimming pools and deep water

Another clear danger is deep water. German Shepherds might be naturally good swimmers, but never leave your puppy by a pool or any deep water unsupervised until you are sure he knows how, and is more than able, to get out.

If you have a pool, it's important to teach him where the shallowest step or exit is and how to get there. The best way to do this is to lift him into this part of the pool with you and show him how to jump out. Gradually he can learn to get back to the step (or exit point) from further away.

Some owners invest in a dog life jacket and teach their puppies how to swim right away, but unless there is real danger of falling in, it would be wise to wait until he is at least three to six months old (keeping him under strict supervision when near the pool).

Tying up

Absolutely not. Please don't ever tie your puppy out in the garden or yard, or on a trolley line. It's unthinkable that if you're reading this book you would consider this an option, but just in case, tying a dog up in the yard would make him frustrated, deeply unhappy, aggressive and even neurotic. Sanity aside, it would put him at risk of hurting his neck or choking; prevent him from escaping from unpredictable danger, such as other dogs, fire or flooding; or simply from seeking shelter from fearful situations like loud bangs, or thunder and lightning.

12. THE FIRST WEEK

From just three weeks old your puppy has been socialising and learning to play with his mother and litter mates. Now suddenly he must learn to be with you, and with people, and to figure out a whole new set of rules. Luckily for you he is at his most impressionable during these early days, so the time and effort you put in now to building a positive relationship will be worth buckets of good behaviour over the months and years to come.

Mesmerisingly cute as he is, your gorgeous bundle of innocence needs to know his position in the household. He needs to understand straight away that you are the leader, and a strong one at that, or there will come a time when he is walking all over you and making the decisions.

We will look at discipline and obedience training later on but until you've read those, if he does something you don't want him to do, don't punish him or show aggression in any form. That would only confuse him and make him fearful of you.

Instead, distract him and encourage him into doing something good. Then reward him for listening. Encourage and reward – praise him at every opportunity for the good things he does in your eyes, so he can begin to learn what is right in your world.

Be clear and consistent in your praise and he will

become the most doting and loyal friend you could ever imagine.

Love him

Unconditionally. Do this and the rest will come naturally.

Teach him his name

Use his name to get his attention, and reward him when he responds to it. But be careful not to say it over and over again or he will quickly become de-sensitised to it.

Make his special place appealing

Associations with the crate or his special place must be positive, so it should never be used for punishment. Make it comfortable and leave toys and treats inside so that it always feels welcoming and homely.

If he has soiled in it, be sure to clean it well.

Encourage him into this space and praise him when he uses it.

Feed and water him

Your puppy should be having three to four meals a day at this stage, ideally of the same food he was having with the other puppies in the litter. If you don't know how much to feed him, work out his daily allowance from the instructions on the food packaging. Split this allowance into three of four portions and work out a schedule for regular feeding, for example:

- Three feeds: 7am, 12.30pm and 6pm
- Four feeds: 7am, 11am, 3pm and 7pm.

(Make sure the last meal of the day is a good two hours before bedtime so that he's less likely to mess in the house during the night.)

If he's on dry puppy food, you can add a little warm water and let it soak for a few minutes before feeding him. This makes it easier to eat and digest.

Water should always be available. If it runs out he'll start looking for alternatives and you don't want him heading for the toilet bowl. German Shepherds that live indoors are great training for owners who don't keep the lid down.

And the water should be fresh. Don't cheat by just topping it up. Empty the bowl, scrub it clean and refill it every day.

REMINDER
*Never let him get hold of
anything listed in the previous
chapter: 'Danger alert!'*

Manage toilet time

Remember that your puppy needs regular toilet breaks and it's up to you to help him with the when and where.

During the day, take him outside every hour if you can, and lead him to the spot you'd most like him to use. When he does it there, make sure he understands that was a good thing by making a HUGE fuss of him. Give him a treat and tell him what a brilliant, amazing, spectacular dog he is.

At night, he won't want to go to the toilet in his special place but when he is very little he can only hold on for so long, so ideally you should be getting up during the night to take him out, as well as early each morning.

"But what about when he does mess inside?" you ask. What of it? He's a baby. Clean up well and be extremely patient. No matter what you've heard or read until now, don't punish him. He won't understand. (There's a whole chapter on toilet training coming up soon.)

Visit the vet

Regulations vary from country to country, but take his vaccination certificate with you and your vet will advise you on what your puppy needs and when. Most vaccines require several rounds, between six weeks and 16 weeks, so scheme these in during this first visit.

Be sure to tell the vet if you have plans to take your puppy to puppy classes or boarding kennels, because either of these require further inoculation.

Get advice on deworming, and the prevention of parasites.

If your puppy has not already been microchipped, it's advisable to have that done now too.

If your puppy's baby nails are very long and catching on everything, you could ask the vet or a veterinary nurse to clip them for you, or to show you how to do it yourself.

Make the visit fun for your puppy by giving him praise and attention, staying by his side when he gets his shots, and telling him how good he is. Possibly take him for a walk or give him a treat afterwards to create a positive association.

Handle him

Your puppy needs to learn that he is safe with people, that they mean him no harm, and that he has no reason to fear them or react defensively.

He should start learning this straight away through lots of physical contact. Pet him and handle him: fondle his paws, move his legs, run your hand over his tail, feel his ears, touch his nose, gently examine his teeth, rub his tummy, groom him, bath him, pick him up and carry him around.

Play with him

Spend lots of time playing with him. And even now – in the post-vaccination days when he should stay inside your property – encourage him to experience the world through different surfaces. Put him on floor tiles, wood, carpet, grass, sand, rock, soft cushions, paper and blankets. Let him get used to them all.

Give him quiet time

He needs some time on his own too so he can learn not to be anxious later on when you aren't there or able to play with him. (See 'Time alone' in the next chapter.) Shut him in his special place for an hour, once or twice a day. If you have a garden or back yard, let him outside without you, or just with your other dogs, for ten minutes every now and then.

Loosen his collar

Check the fit of his collar every few days. He is growing fast and it'll need to be loosened regularly. Remember that you should be able to fit two fingers between the collar and his neck.

13. EIGHT TO ELEVEN WEEKS

FRAGILE! HANDLE WITH CARE!

Your puppy is weaning himself from his mother and you need to be ultra-sensitive to his feelings. Of course, you should always be sensitive to his feelings, but this is the worst time for anything to frighten him! Luckily for you, German Shepherds are the most fearless of dogs, but don't let this lull you into being a less-attentive puppy parent. The time from eight to approximately eleven or twelve weeks is known as the 'fear period' for all breeds and, yes, even for Shepherds. It is a stage when puppies are over-sensitive and when negative stimuli are the most likely to leave a lasting impression. For example, a loud electric storm when your pup is all alone could lead to a lifelong fear of storms.

But this is also a time of opportunity. If he's already afraid of something, it's a good time to try to recondition him. For example, if he's afraid of umbrellas, show him that you are not afraid of them. Handle them gently in his presence without pressuring him in any way.

And from eight to eleven weeks is a particularly good

time to show your puppy that most experiences are harmless. The more you expose him to the real world now, the more confidence he will have going forward.

SOCIALISATION

The best way to help your puppy adjust to his new life in your world is to socialise him when he still young. You will be able to teach him fancy dog tricks for years, but these next few weeks are the most important for getting him out and about. Use them well and don't let them slip by.

Socialising means introducing him to as many people and animals of all shapes, colours and sizes as possible. Visit friends and have friends to visit him. If puppy parties and puppy training are on offer in your area, take him along. (The chapter 'Stepping out' looks at how to do this safely and considerately.)

HABITUATION

He should also be exposed to as many new places and conditions as possible. In all fairness, you can't shut him indoors then expect him to behave normally around new people, places and things.

Take him with you everywhere you can and let him explore. Let him discover different smells, surfaces, sounds and sights. Take him into a park, to the school gates, for a walk along a river, go to a sports match, go to the shops, paddle through puddles. Walk him over and under bridges. Let him see cars and trucks and trains and planes. Thunder, lightning and snow might be hard to arrange, but ideally let him experience different weather conditions too. Take him out at night and in the rain.

Feeling safe

It is imperative though that during these new experiences he feels safe as well as having fun. Helping him to feel at ease in new situations will go a long way towards helping him grow up to be a happy and well-adjusted dog, so stay with him through these new discoveries and don't let any of them frighten or over-excite him. Going forward, he can only be properly receptive to your training when he is feeling confident and secure.

Here are some ideas to help with this.

- If you come across a potentially frightening situation – some big kids playing rough and tumble at the park for example – watch him closely for signs of discomfort. If he is hiding between your legs, or tucking his tail between his legs, you should back off and find a different route.
- Never put him under pressure to get close to anyone or anything.
- Be alert and sensitive to his feelings, so you will know when you can approach and when to stay away. There are many signs which mean different

things in different contexts. (See the chapter 'Puppy-People Translator').

- If you are not sure how he feels, avoid having a tight lead, so he knows he has a choice. If he is curious, approach from a distance. Let him look, listen and smell, gradually closing the distance as he is comfortable.
- You might want to pick him up and let him watch from your arms, but always be there for him as a reassuring presence.

Accidental noise

Don't forget about background noises that you are accustomed to but might well frighten your puppy.

TV and radio – Be especially alert during this time to sounds on TV or the radio. Dogs barking aggressively in a chase involving hounds, for example, could leave him terrified. Turn the sound down or off if he becomes alarmed – and before then if possible.

Tension in the house – Keep a good vibe in the house. If he hears angry voices or senses a bad mood, he won't understand that it has nothing to do with him (whether it does or not).

Fireworks and thunder – Close doors and windows, and muffle the sound with your own music or voices. Stay close to your puppy, showing him that you are not afraid.

TIME ALONE

Dogs owners are increasingly aware of their dogs' need to be socialised and exposed to everything, and many go to great lengths to arrange this exposure. But just as many owners forget that being alone is one of these experiences. In fact giving your puppy time alone is giving him one of his most essential life skills.

Dogs are social and don't like being alone, but most of them **have** to be alone at some time or another and the best way to minimise or even prevent separation anxiety at a later stage is to start leaving your puppy on his own now, just occasionally, during the day. If he is lucky enough to be right by your side for most of the time this is even more important. As with all his training, start practising this slowly.

- Choose a time when he is getting tired and likely to sleep soon.
- Take him outside for a little play and a toilet break.
- Shut him in his crate or special place with everything he needs.
- Ignore any whining and leave the room or go out for a short while.
- If he is very little and goes to sleep while you are out, open the crate door when you return so he can get out when he wakes.
- Start off with about ten minutes and build it up slowly to no more than an hour at this stage. For one thing, he will be needing the toilet.

BARKING

It's especially important not to punish barking between eight and eleven weeks of age for all the reasons we've considered. Your puppy should be allowed to explore and to express himself.

If he is barking because he is worried about something, and you know that fear is unfounded, lead him away from it and give him a treat. Reassure him with a gentle voice, then gradually expose him to whatever it is that he is afraid of, showing him that you are with him, that you are not afraid and that there is nothing to worry about.

AGGRESSION

Handling your puppy lots and often while he is very young is an excellent way to prevent him from developing aggressive behaviour later on. Teach him now that you can hold and touch him, his toys and his food whenever and however you please.

How?

By doing just that. Handle him, his toys and his food whenever and however you please. (Refer to the section on handling in the previous chapter.) That way he is less likely to become territorial and possessive over what he considers to be his things.

There is always a reason for aggression, and it is usually founded on fear and insecurity. But whatever the cause, it is unacceptable towards you and others.

SMALL CHILDREN

It is widely accepted that having a dog as a cherished member of the family is good for children's emotional development. But small children need to be taught how to behave around your puppy, and they must be supervised when they play with him.

Put yourself in your puppy's paws and imagine being picked up continually, carried around, possibly even dropped, pestered, woken up ... Imagine what it would be like not to be able to say, 'I don't want to play any more'. The only way your puppy or dog knows to tell someone they're hurting, tired, frightened or have had enough is to growl or snap. And the best way for you to manage this is to not make your puppy have to do this from the start.

The following points are reiterated from the chapter 'The homecoming' where we first talk about the importance of teaching small children that your puppy is NOT a toy.

- They should not be allowed to pick him up.
- They should not be allowed to disturb him if he is sleeping or has taken himself to a quiet place.
- They should not run around squealing, and if the puppy becomes over-excited they should be calm and still.
- They should be allowed to play calm games, but nothing involving wrestling or tugging.
- They should stay on their feet while playing, because if they writhe on the ground with the puppy, the puppy is likely to treat them like his litter mates and mouth and bite.

NOTE
If your puppy starts developing a habit
of growling menacingly at you or your child,
call in a dog behavioural expert.

FURTHER CRATE TRAINING

If you are using a crate and it started off at your bedside overnight, you should move it further from the bedroom – step by step if you like – to its permanent day-time position in the house. But only do this as your puppy grows in confidence and don't rush it. Your job is to build his trust.

If your puppy is going to be in the crate for a lengthy period while you are out, then you should leave him with some food as well as his water and toys.

FEEDING

What?

It's common for dogs to be hugely enthusiastic about a particular food the first few times they try it and then suddenly change their minds. Don't buy more than one bag at a time so that if he's lost interest in it by the end of the bag you can soon let him try another brand. Mealtimes will always be high-points in your dog's day, so it's only right that you shop around for a food he loves.

Change of food

If you are changing your puppy's food, incorporate the new brand slowly.

For example, for two to three days give him one quarter of the daily allowance of the new food with three quarters of the daily allowance of the old. A few days later make it half of one with half of the other, again for a few days, then increase the new food to three quarters and finally the full meal.

There's a baffling array of dog food brands and flavours on the market, so if you're making this decision without the advice of the breeder or your vet, make sure you choose a high-quality food that is appropriate for his age. This is because puppies and adolescents need higher levels of both protein and fat in their diets than adult dogs. It's also worth noting here that although dogs prefer meat-based to plant-based foods, a balanced meal is one that combines both.

As a guide, many German Shepherd owners feed their dogs on a diet of three parts dry food to one part wet (or canned) food, and then supplement this with chews and treats.

Reminders

- Don't give your puppy scraps from the table.
- Don't let him con you into giving him more food than his daily allowance.
- Don't let him get hold of anything listed in the chapter 'Danger alert!'.

COLLAR

Check daily that his collar is not getting too tight. He is growing fast and it'll need to be loosened regularly. Remember, you should be able to insert two fingers between the collar and his neck.

GROOMING

Brushing

There's no stopping your German Shepherd from shedding … and shedding. So if there's a part of your house you want to keep fur free, the only real way to achieve this is to keep that area totally off-limits to your dog. But you can cut down on the shedding with regular brushing – 'regular' meaning anything from daily to at least once a week.

But there's lots of good news too:
- A German Shepherd's coat seldom gets knotty or matted, and the dirt usually just falls right off it.
- There's no need for the grooming parlour (just a couple of brushes and you're good to go).
- Your dog will love being groomed and what's more brushing strengthens the bond between you.
- It also keeps his skin healthy and helps you to pick up on any lumps, sores or parasites.
- And it is very good for teaching your dog to be handled, especially during vet visits.

To help your puppy get used to grooming, start with a brush with soft bristles, and have very short sessions in case he's getting restless. It's quite normal for him to want to mouth the brush at first, so be patient with him. He will soon learn to enjoy this time with you.

When he is older and his coat is thicker you can also use a stiffer brush with fine, bent wires, as these are better for shedding the soft undercoat.

Washing

Because your puppy's natural oils are keeping his skin and his coat healthy, you should avoid bathing him too often. (Even when he is older he shouldn't need more than four or five baths a year.) He does need to learn about baths while he is little though – and it's so much easier to handle a puppy than his ninety-pound adult self – but try to keep the number of puppy baths down too, to no more than one a month.

Indoor baths

- Use your own bath or a washtub. If you're using the bath, place a non-skid mat on the bottom.
- It's also advisable to put a strainer over the plug hole to prevent his hair from clogging up the drain.
- Use a quality dog shampoo, have towels at the ready, and wear old clothes and a good sense of humour because you **will** get wet..
- Ease him into the bath or washtub, offering lots of praise and treats.
- Run luke-warm water over him (ideally with a hand-held sprayer) before soaking him with a wet sponge.
- Rub in the shampoo and lather, then rinse several times, working the shampoo out with your hands.
- Bathe his head last because this is when he will shake the most. And avoid spraying water in his ears.
- Wrap him in a towel before he shakes too much and rub him down thoroughly.
- German Shepherds' coats take an age to dry, so if you can get him used to a hair dryer, they are really helpful. Start a little at a time and blow in the direction of his coat. And NEVER use a dryer on a hot setting – always cool or slightly warm, and tested on yourself first.

- When his coat is almost, but not completely, dry is an excellent time to give him a good brush because a lot of hair will be loose from the wash.

Outdoor washes

On hot summer's days you might prefer to wash him outside. You will need a hosepipe and a clean surface that won't get muddy. You will most likely also need a helper to hold him for you. Either that or a space where he can't run off.

TIPS

- *Dilute the shampoo with water. This will make it go further **and** make it easier to work into a lather.*

- *Holding a hand over the base of one ear will prevent him from shaking all over you. But step right back when you let go.*

Nails

Your puppy needs his nails, but if they get unmanageably long they will need clipping. Perhaps you had this done at his first vet visit, but if not, and you feel confident enough to do it yourself, you can buy your own clippers. With your dog standing up, pick up a foot so that it bends naturally. Holding it in your empty hand, look for the part of the nail you can see through if you hold a light to his paw. You want to avoid the 'quick', which is inside the nail and contains sensitive nerve endings. Clip a tiny bit at a time, inspecting after each clip to make sure there is no bleeding. If you want, you can file the nails smooth with an emery board.

Teeth

There are lots of treats on the market that double as dental chews to clean your puppy's teeth and keep his gums healthy. If you want to clean his teeth and to clean them by brushing, you can buy dog toothbrushes and meat-flavoured pastes.

TRAINING

This isn't a now-and-then exercise reserved for obedience classes. It's an ongoing, moment-by-moment process that starts the minute your puppy enters your life. Training is about mutual understanding, clear communication and a better life for your puppy as well as everyone else in the family. This means that every member of the family and household should be involved, using the same set of rules, spoken commands and body language.

The chapters 'Behaviour' and 'Training' cover the key DOs and DON'Ts to help you build a strong foundation for a relationship based on understanding and respect.

PLAYTIME

This doesn't mean putting your puppy outside with his toys. Play is social interaction. So you, or a member of the family, needs to actually play with him. In fact playtime is so important that there's a full chapter devoted to this too, with key pointers to help you make every game and every play session a positive experience. The chapter also has ideas for toys and games, and it won't take long for you to figure out his favourites as well as the games you play best together.

EXERCISE

All dogs need exercise, so they don't get bored, unruly, overweight or unhealthy. Your full-grown German Shepherd will need an hour to two hours of exercise a day, but between eight and eleven weeks of age take your puppy on two to three walks a day of no more than 10-15 minutes at a time. As a rough guide, add five minutes to the length of each walk per month, so that by four months, he should ideally have walks of approximately 20 minutes each. As a rule, more shorter walks are better for puppies than fewer longer ones.

The chapter 'Stepping out' is full of advice and tips for your outings.

NOTE

Puppies grow up fast compared with human children. One week in your puppy's life is equivalent to around five months' development in a human child.

14. TWELVE WEEKS PLUS

Although at twelve weeks your puppy is still heavily dependent on you and ever so eager to please, he will start leaving your side to explore more. You will still be on his radar all the time, but you will begin to stop tripping over him whenever you step backwards.

His socialisation is still incredibly important and should be ongoing. As for chewing, he will be munching on everything.

Teething

By twelve weeks, your puppy's adult teeth, a full 42 of them, are waiting to push out those super-sharp baby teeth. It then takes until around 18 weeks for those baby teeth to even start falling out. That's a lot of weeks of important chewing to be done so – for the sake of your puppy, your house and your sanity – keep valuables out of reach, and always have an abundant and ready supply of toys and treats that he **is** allowed to chew on.

We will look at chewing again under 'Discipline'.

Ear pointing

When your puppy has finished with teething, his ears should begin their delightful fight against the flop. They will flip endearingly and independently between floppy and upright until the cartilage has strengthened enough to keep them standing up. All puppies develop differently, but the floppy-to-pointed-ear stage is usually between five and seven months of age.

Sleep

By this age, your puppy no longer needs the 18-22 hours' sleep he needed when you brought him home, but he does still need a good 16 hours of rest or sleep a day.

Food

Twelve weeks to six months: If you've been feeding your puppy four times a day, then by twelve weeks you can cut this back to three times a day. Divide his daily food allowance (according to the instructions on the pack) into three portions instead of four and alter your schedule for regular feeding to, for example, 7am, 12.30pm and 6pm. And remember to avoid feeding too close to your bedtime, so he's less likely to mess in the house or his crate during the night.

Six months to a year: By six months you can gradually bring the meals down to twice a day, which is how often he will need feeding as an adult dog.

Overfeeding: Research studies show that rapid growth increases the likelihood of a dog's developing hip dysplasia. Because German Shepherds are prone to this problem, some owners switch their puppies to a food with lower protein levels (20-25%) at about 12 weeks. The puppy will then grow more slowly but still reach the expected adult size. Make a mental note now, however, not to let your Shepherd get underweight or overweight at any stage of his life. These dogs are athletes and are meant to be lean as well as strong and muscular.

The following chapters (right up to 'Puppy-People Translator') focus on the most important and pressing puppy issues in terms of behaviour and training, and are filled with tips to help you as you guide your little one into adolescence and beyond.

15. BEHAVIOUR

Your puppy loves you so much! He wants to learn from you and please you. But he only knows what his survival instincts tell him, so, to reiterate, it's your job to teach him what is and isn't allowed in your world.

We will look at specific behaviours in the next chapters, but the pointers in this general chapter are fundamental to all of these.

For a well-behaved puppy, the first thing to understand – as you surely do by now – is that puppies are much more receptive when they have nothing to fear. A fearful puppy will never be totally engaged.

Our understanding of animal behaviour is improving all the time, and it's no longer acceptable to punish dogs, never mind puppies, by shouting, smacking and rubbing their noses in the carpet. This sort of treatment is both ineffective and counterproductive. It scares your puppy and puts you in a bad mood. You lose your dog's trust and the spinout of that – into all the other areas of the relationship – is just not worth thinking about. You want your puppy to be happy and optimistic, looking forward to everything, rather than fearing it.

So how do you achieve this? In a nutshell: you gain his trust by focusing on the things he does right. By encouraging good behaviour and rewarding it!

Encourage and reward

Always tell him what you DO want him to do, rather than what you DON'T want him to do. Let's say for example he's got the TV remote between his teeth. Don't shout and get angry! Calmly distract him with something else, something he IS allowed to chew on. Refocus him on this new and exciting toy, and rescue the remote. If you don't have anything at hand, then ask him to do something to obey you – even something as simple as a 'Sit!'

His feelings are everything

Let's say your puppy bounds up to you with a glint in his eye, a wag in his tail and a captured, dishevelled bathmat in his mouth. Try not to think about your favourite bathmat which, after all, is just a thing and has no feelings at all! Instead, think about HOW HE'S FEELING about what he's done. He thinks he's done brilliantly, doesn't he? He wants a medal. Scold him now and you'll really confuse him. Then again, if you praise him, he might keep bringing you bathmat-type presents ad infinitum. So what do you do?

You don't scold or praise. Distract him instead by calling him to you and getting his attention onto something else, a toy perhaps. When he is refocused on the toy, offer him a tempting chew. By then the bathmat should be far from his mind, and you should be able to rescue it. And if it's still functional, remember to hang it up out of his puppy-jaw reach for a few months.

You are the leader

To establish a positive relationship, your puppy must understand from the start that, even though you love him and you are best friends, your word is law and he must listen to you. And he will, as long as you are a worthy leader and a good teacher.

Here are some key tips for you.

- Don't be aggressive towards him. Instead, be gentle but firm.
- Don't go too easy on him either. In the long run that can be as unfair as punishing him.
- Be crystal clear in your instructions. Use single words rather than sentences and try to be consistent in your choice of words. Don't switch between 'Come!' and 'Here!' for example, or 'Walk!' and 'Heel!'.

- Keep your tone positive.
- Use body language as well as verbal commands.
- When he does what you want, show him unreservedly how clever he is. Be happy and excited and reward him with praise.

Timing is all-important

It's vital that you teach your puppy with timely signals – signals that apply to what he is doing AT THAT TIME. If you discipline him for something he did two minutes ago, he won't understand the reason. For example, if he runs off after a cat and then comes back, and you shout at him for chasing the cat as he is coming back, he will naturally think you are shouting at him for coming back and not for chasing the cat. The result? He is confused and intimidated, and next time he will think twice about coming back. Too many well-meaning dog owners make the mistake of misplaced timing – and it's simply unfair.

Prevent bad behaviour

- Try to anticipate things that might go wrong. If you think he's about to chase the cat, hold on to him and distract him with a toy. Billowing tablecloths, for example, are begging for trouble. Don't use them until he's older.
- Make sure his basic needs are met: love, food, water, warmth, things to chew on, sleep, play, exercise and exploration. If he has all of these he is far less likely to behave badly in the first place.
- Don't put temptation in his way. If you don't want him eating from your dinner plate, don't leave it lying around, unattended and in easy reach. That would just be setting him up to fail.

Let him know when you disapprove

In many bad behaviours, the best way to tell your puppy you don't like what he's doing is to take away something he wants – your attention. Discourage bad behaviour by ignoring him when he is behaving in any way that is not acceptable to you. Stop play, walk away, look away, leave the room if you can.

When to say 'No!' or 'Leave!'

1. When your puppy does something totally unacceptable, something that could endanger his life for example.

2. When he boldly ignores your voice command because he would rather do something else.

These need to be corrected immediately and here's how.

- Reprimand him straight away. Say 'NO!' or 'LEAVE!' in a voice that is loud and startling enough to prevent or stop his behaviour. It should be in stark contrast to your usual quiet and calm voice, and used sparingly for best effect.
- Block his way with your body, or physically stop him if you need to.
- Then make eye contact and use your voice to get him to focus on you.
- Once you have his attention, praise him for changing his focus.
- The trouble with 'No' and 'Leave' is that your puppy doesn't know what he's meant to do instead. Always try to give him something better to do or to chew on.

Still struggling?

If you've tried all these things with a bad behaviour, with repeated, clear and consistent communication, and you're still struggling, you can resort to time-out. Shut him in the kitchen, or a similar and safe place, and leave him for a few minutes – five is acceptable, ten is too long.

Alternatively, you can tie him up in a safe and suitable time-out spot, and ignore him for five minutes. (Never go out and leave him like that.) The lead should be just long enough for him to be able to sit up and lie down comfortably.

Rules must be consistent

We've been here before, but this is **really** important. If one person lets your puppy onto the sofa, it's downright unfair for someone else to reprimand him for being there. Rules will be very confusing if they differ from person to person, so it's really crucial that everyone in your puppy's life understands and teaches what is and what isn't allowed in precisely the same way.

Serious behavioural problems

In my experience German Shepherds are gentle dogs but, given their size and reputation as police and war dogs, many people are afraid of them. In fairness to these people, Shepherds are big and powerful and boast impressive sets of gnashers. But this only means it is all the more important that they do not develop any aggressive behaviours, including:

- growling or biting in response to punishment or
- because they are being possessive over food or toys.

It is also important here that you are able to tell the difference between playfulness and aggression. See the chapter 'Puppy-People Translator' for clues on reading the signs.

If your puppy develops any traits that could endanger you, himself, or any other person or their dog, you should get help from a professional in dog behaviour. And the same goes for any other serious behavioural issue.

Let's look at some common behavioural issues in more detail.

16. JUMPING UP

Your puppy will jump up because he is happy to see you, because he loves you, because he wants to lick you all over your face and he can't reach, because he wants you to pet him and play with him. Although he is used to jumping up on his mother and litter mates, he now needs to learn not to jump up on you or other people. You might not mind his jumping up right now – after all he is not likely to bowl anyone over with his loving greetings while he is such a little tyke – but when he is a big, heavy adult he could easily send someone flying.

And size aside, don't forget about muddy paws and sharp claws. Basically, jumping up soon becomes a nuisance and you want to nip it in the bud **before** it gets out of hand. So …

Don't
- Reward him for jumping up
- Talk to him
- Tell him to get down
- Push him away
- Shout or yell
- Smack him or use physical punishment of any sort.

Do
- Step back so that his paws don't reach you
- Look away from him
- Turn away from him

- Lift your hands away and don't touch him
- After a few seconds, come back to him, and repeat if necessary
- When he has quietened down and stopped jumping, be sure to praise him and reward him.
- Get all family members to do this, and ask regular visitors to help with this too.
- If jumping up on visitors is likely, put him on a lead before opening the door to them.

How does it work?

This method will eventually teach him that if he jumps up he will get no attention, and that if he keeps his four paws on the ground he will be praised.

17. TOILET TRAINING

Remember, at first he has no idea that the house is not a public toilet. This is something you need to teach him – and with time and patience.

In a nutshell, initially you will need to take him outside hourly and show him where to go. When he does go in an acceptable place, and as soon as he has finished his business, it's time to celebrate. Reward! Reward! Reward! That way you will teach him that doing his business outside means AMAZING things will happen.

Here are some key DOs and DON'Ts to help speed up the process.

Do

- When your puppy arrives at your house for the first time, give him a guided tour. The sooner he understands that all this space is living area, the sooner he will stop using it as a toilet.
- Take him outside every hour.
- Also take him outside immediately if you spot any of these tell-tale signs:
  - Sniffing and circling the floor
  - Whining
  - Pacing up and down
  - Scratching the floor.

- Lead him to the spot you'd like to encourage him to use.
- Then wait. And wait some more. Stay out there with him – come rain or shine – watching him all the time.
- You can spur him on with an encouraging command, like 'quickly now' or 'wee time'.
- Wait until he's completely finished before you reward him, or he might only do half his business.
- As soon as he **is** finished, shower him with praise.
- When he goes to the toilet inside, thoroughly clean the place he's marked and use a pet-safe odour eliminator. Your puppy is most likely to go to the toilet somewhere he can already smell wee or poop, so the best way is to teach him where to make his messes is to keep your house clean. (If possible, limit your puppy's access to carpeted areas.)
- If he has messed inside but on a training mat or piece of newspaper, carry this outside to where you'd like him to go in future, and weigh it down there with something heavy so it can't blow away. The smell will act as a signal to him to do his business there.

Don't

- Punish him for piddling or pooping inside. Punishing him for something he can't help and doesn't fully understand would only make him nervous and slow his progress.
- Leave him outside on his own. He will just turn his attention to getting back to you, and when he does get back inside the house, he will very likely still need to go.

How long will toilet training take?

German Shepherds are renowned for being easy to housetrain. Progress obviously varies from puppy to puppy, but it's safe to assume he will leave the odd surprise for you until he's around six months of age, and it could take up to a year for him to be accident free. Be patient.

NOTES

- *Your puppy will never wee or poop to spite you.*
- *Some dogs make a little wee as a sign of submission, and some wee with excitement. These lapses should never be punished!*

TIP

Once your puppy understands that you want him to do his toiletries outside, you can hang a bell on a string from the door that leads to outside. He might well learn to jingle the bell to tell you when he needs to go out.

18. MOUTHING AND NIPPING

All dogs love to play, and play involves mouthing one another, so it's completely natural for your puppy to want to play bite. He might also bite because he is teething. If, like many new puppy owners, you don't mind your puppy chewing your hands now, you soon will. As he gets older, the biting will get harder and involve others too, so he should learn as soon as possible not to use his teeth on people.

Adult dogs are good at controlling the pressure of their jaws, but puppies often make the mistake of biting too hard because they are still learning and practising jaw control. If a puppy bites one of its litter mates too hard while playing, the hurt puppy will yelp and stop playing. Your puppy has already learned from the other puppies that biting too hard inhibits play time.

He will learn gradually to play more gently until he understands not to let his teeth into contact with your skin at all.

Do

- Play with him with a chew toy in your hand. If he bites you and inflicts pain, make a high yelping sound and immediately withdraw your hand. This is exactly what would have happened with his litter mates, so it will help him to learn that it's okay to nip the chew toy, but not your hand.

- If the biting persists, remove yourself from the game, the room even, just for a few minutes to show him that teeth on skin equals no more playing. It's not a quick fix, but he will gradually make the association.
- Supervise small children. Their tendency when a puppy mouths them is to scream and run around, which only excites and encourages the puppy even more.

Don't

- Shout at him or smack him if he mouths or nips. This can make the biting harder to control.
- Rush him. He must learn jaw control gradually and through experience.
- Play rough tug games – they just encourage biting.

19. CHEWING HOUSE AND HOME

*'Puppies are constantly inventing new ways to
be bad. It's fascinating. You come into a room
they've been in and see pieces of debris and try
to figure out what you had that was made from
wicker or what had been stuffed with fluff'*
Julie Klam

All dogs chew, especially puppies! They chew things
either because they are teething or simply to explore.
Chewing is how they learn about the world around
them – they don't have hands, so they inspect
everything they can with their mouths and teeth.

Your puppy will chew on anything he can, so it's
really important to give him things you **are** happy for
him to chew on.

Don't

- Leave valuable and tempting chewables, like shoes,
  lying around on the floor. Puppies are excellent
  training for untidy owners.
- Encourage sticks. They can splinter and get stuck
  in his mouth.
- If you find your puppy chewing something he
  shouldn't, don't try to take it away from him, and
  especially don't start a tug-of-war.

Do

- Instead of trying to pull or coax it away from him, replace it with something he **is** allowed to chew on – and make sure this replacement offering is something you know he loves. As he plays with the forbidden item, hold the new and better offering to his nose and say, 'Leave!', 'Drop!' or 'Off!'
- When he drops it, you can give him the treat and a pat.
- Make sure you have lots of puppy toys and treats. (Pet toys are created to appeal to your dog by smell, taste, feel and shape, but you can also use old soft toys.)
- Keep these prizes close by; you never know when you'll be needing them.
- If you see him approaching something with demolition on his mind, call him with a happy voice. Puppies are easily distracted, and he should immediately forget what he'd planned to do and come running to you. Reward him for coming and give him something more suitable to get his teeth into.
- If your puppy's got a taste for something that can't be moved – a table leg for example, spray it with a pet-friendly anti-chew, or citronella.

TIP
Tie a knot in an old sock
and give it to him as a toy.
He'll think he's the luckiest
dog on the planet.

When will it end?

Your puppy's need to gnaw on everything in sight will go away, but it won't be overnight. In fact, it will probably take well over a year.

20. DIGGING

It's absolutely natural for German Shepherds to dig.
That's not to say your puppy will, because not all
German Shepherds do. But if your puppy does take too
much of a liking to digging, here's what to do:

- Find him a place where he IS allowed to dig.
- Bury things for him in that spot and let him find
  them.
- Then, if you find him digging in other places, tell
  him 'No!' or 'Leave!', fill the hole he has made back
  up, and show him again where he can and should
  dig instead.

SOMETHING TO TRY

*If the problem persists, make an unpleasant
clanging noise whenever you see him starting to dig.
Hit a pot with a metal spoon for example.
Soon he'll associate digging – either in that place or
altogether – with this horrible noise.*

21. BARKING

Your German Shepherd puppy will bark for very good reason, no reason at all, just for fun, to make suggestions ... and sometimes even to make demands.

Barking at others

It's natural for him to warn you about strangers or intruders, and that kind of barking is not necessarily something you want to stop or even discourage. Let him bark at them, just momentarily, then call him back to you and praise him, or distract him with a toy or an exercise if you need to.

But if your puppy is barking at a passer by – or the neighbour's cat, which is more likely at this stage – and you **do** want him to stop, your instinct is probably to shout at him to keep quiet. But put yourself in his shoes and you will see that if you shout at him while he is barking, he is likely to interpret your shouting as 'people barking', and think you are egging him on, or even coming to help. The result? He will bark even harder.

So with unwanted barking, as with pretty much all bad behaviour, it's more effective to give him the 'I'm ignoring you now!' treatment.

- Don't talk to him or touch him
- Instead turn away from him
- Leave the room or area if you can

- If he won't stop barking and it's becoming a problem, you could distract him with a loud noise (like hitting a pot with a metal spoon)
- When he has settled down and come to you, you can acknowledge and reward him for his new-found quiet behaviour.

Barking at you

As your puppy comes to see that efforts to win your attention, like jumping up or nipping, are fruitless, he might well replace these with his latest greatest trick – an ear-piercing yap that says:

- I am still here.
- Stop ignoring me.
- Hey, I want some of that too.
- Come on, let's play.
- Pick me up …

Whatever it is, he wants your attention. Don't give it to him. Instead, pull out your now-well-practised ignoring techniques:

- Look away and turn away
- Don't talk to him
- Lift your hands away and don't touch him
- Leave the room if you can.

But, as always, when he has quietened down,
be sure to acknowledge and reward him.

Incessant barking

You should NEVER leave your puppy alone for a long time! Left on his own for long periods, even a mature German Shepherd is likely to bark because he is lonely, frustrated, bored or needs attention.

If he is shut up in a small space or worse, tied up, he will bark incessantly too, and who could blame him?

Do

- Move him to a less isolated place.
- Arrange for there to be more space for him to play in.
- Take him for long or longer walks.
- Give him more time to interact with you and other dogs.
- Being left at home alone all day is hard on any dog, but German Shepherds really are pack animals. They need company and one of the simplest solutions would be to get another dog.

Don't

- Leave your puppy alone in small spaces for long periods in the first place. It's simply not fair.

22. STEPPING OUT

Once your puppy has been fully vaccinated you can
start walking him out and taking him on outings. But
first he needs to practise walking on the lead at home
and while you're waiting for his vaccinations to take
effect is the ideal time.

Eventually you want him walking by your side on
a loose lead, but for a puppy, with seemingly endless
stores of pent-up energy, this is surprisingly difficult to
learn.

Do

- Use a normal collar (no choke chains) and a six-foot
  non-extendable lead.
- Attach the lead when he is calm and not resisting
  you.
- Start by letting him wander around the house with
  the lead trailing behind him, but try not to let him
  chew it.
- The next stage is to pick up the lead and encourage
  him to walk along beside you.
- If he pulls, stand still and call him to you. Praise
  him, then try again.
- When he is walking nicely alongside you, with the
  lead slack but off the ground, reward him
  generously with praise and treats.

Don't

- Use a choke chain or half check.
- Drag him. That would only make him panic and pull away.
- Be pulled along by him. That would teach him that pulling works in his favour.
- If he is pulling, don't pull back, or yank on the lead, or shout at him. Instead, stop and call him to you and praise him for coming.

When the time comes for him to get out and about, here are a few things to consider and be aware of.

Safety

Think carefully about where you're going to take him so you can avoid frightening or stressful experiences.

- Choose a safe, open space away from busy roads.
- A place where other dog owners are likely to act in a responsible way.
- And think about the best time to go. Perhaps it's too soon for a Saturday morning at the park if there is likely to be a noisy sports match in play.

If something does scare him on an outing, let him know you are with him, protecting him, and that he is safe.

What to take:

Make sure you have him on his lead (a short one is better to start with) and are armed with:

- Biodegradable poo bags – more than one
- Treats (ideally in a treat pouch) – so you can reward good behaviour
- Water and a bowl – if there is no clean water where you are going. (As a space saver, you might like to invest in a pets' water bottle with a flap or lid that doubles as a bowl.)

Pooping

If he poops, pick it up and dispose of it at home (or in a public dog waste bin if one is provided).

Other dogs

When you come across other dogs on your outings, you could use the opportunity for your puppy to practise his meeting and greeting. But never assume that other people or their dogs are happy to reciprocate. And never let your dog run up to other dogs unless their walkers have told you it's okay. There are lots of reasons why it might not be. Perhaps the dog is very old; maybe it is injured; in recovery; not good with puppies; or the owner is working on a specific training exercise. Always ask first and from a distance:

1. whether their dog is good with puppies and

2. whether they are happy for your puppy to say 'hello'.

If it is okay for your dogs to meet, stay close by to supervise, and to pre-empt any bad experiences.

- Make sure you walk on past some dogs, and people too, so your puppy doesn't take it for granted that he can run up to anyone for a chin-and tail-wag.

Play dates

If your puppy meets another dog he plays especially well with, you could arrange play dates at times that suit you both.

Together time

- Put your smart phone out of temptation's way and make this quality time with your puppy!
- If you are going somewhere with big open spaces like the park, you can take a long, extendable lead. But NEVER pull your puppy back with the line. He should come to you as called. There is more on this in 'Training'.

23. EXERCISE

German Shepherds love running. As an adult, your dog will run and run till YOU drop, and then still want to run some more. So, unless you're a marathon athlete yourself, it'll be up to you to find ways to give him the exercise he needs.

Walking

Walking is fantastic, low-impact exercise for you both. Once your puppy is walking nicely on the lead, you can start picking up the pace, gradually working up to a brisker walk and over longer distances.

Once he's fully grown, he'll need walking several miles a day – half a mile at the very least, and adult German Shepherds make great hiking partners.

Running

Never jog with your puppy because his bones are still forming, but adult Shepherds make fabulous jogging partners too. If you decide to start jogging with him when he is fully-grown then, as with the walking, you would need to work up the distances slowly.

With running you would also need to be mindful of his paws. Dogs aren't well booted like you, so stay away from long stretches of hard ground and be aware of surfaces that might be either very hot, or cold and icy.

Swimming

Swimming is fantastic exercise and many German Shepherds are incorrigible water babies.

If yours wants to give it a go, you'll probably find he starts off trying to walk on the water, lifting his front feet right out with each step. If he does this, a good tip is to hold his bottom up so that his front feet stay underwater. But don't push him into anything he doesn't want to do.

Games and playtime

These also count towards his daily exercise and are especially fantastic for mental stimulation. The chapter 'Playtime' is filled with ideas and tips.

BUT ...

... All of these activities come with their own risks – some obvious and others totally unpredictable, so here is a shortlist of things to be alert to. The list is not meant to have you deprive your puppy or dog of the great outdoors and the exercise he absolutely must have; it's just to help you avoid taking chances with his safety.

On land:

- Even if your puppy or dog is hugely reliable off the lead, blind trust is still careless. Don't let him loose anywhere near traffic – he can cover a lot of ground very quickly and squirrels, rabbits and deer for example could lure him on a merry chase.
- Make sure you know the area well before letting him off the lead – apart from roadways, be aware of cliffs, drainage culverts and thin ice.
- Although your dog might feel like the king of beasts, some animals will get the better of him. As

far as possible, keep him away from porcupines, skunks and snakes.

- Be careful not to let him graze on greenery on hikes. Not all tasty plants are agreeable, or even safe.
- If he's walking along the coast, keep him away from dead fish.

In water:

As a basic rule, if he is swimming take the same precautions with him as you would with a young child.

- Cold water can cause hypothermia, which could drain him of his strength to swim to land.
- In the sea, stay clear of rough waves, undertows and side currents.
- Rivers are dangerous when they are fast-flowing, eddying or moving towards a waterfall or weir.
- Be especially careful of steep banks – natural drops as well as manmade ones on the edges of ditches and canals. Anything he could not easily get out of.
- If it's a swimming pool he's in, make sure he knows where the step is and how to get out.
- In the wild, consider the possibility of other animals in the water: alligators, crocs, sharks, snapping turtles.

24. TRASNING

'Properly trained,
a man can be dog's
best friend'
Corey Ford

You most likely assume that puppy training is about training your puppy – most people do – but in actual fact it is nearly all about you, the owner, learning how to communicate effectively with your puppy.

And puppy training is not about tricks either. To reiterate, it is about basic obedience to improve communication and understanding. Why? For a better quality of life for you, your puppy … and everyone he meets.

Everything from the chapter on Behaviour applies to this chapter too because the premise for training is the same. Because your puppy is more engaged when he has nothing to fear, you should train by encouraging and rewarding good behaviour. Always tell him what you DO want him to do, rather than what you DON'T want him to do.

And training should be fun. The best trained dogs wag their tails during training because they enjoy the challenge as well as the reward.

Reward-based training

Praise is always a motivator in training, but it is often not enough, and it is now commonly accepted that training with food-motivation, at least at first, has the best results. Initially, then, praise is a secondary reinforcer. In time, you can wean your dog from the food-based training, and he will obey you purely for the fun of the training itself. But even then, you should reward him with treats intermittently.

When to start

Training starts the moment you bring your German Shepherd home. And if you've signed up for puppy classes at some future date, don't wait. Teach him what you can, little by little, moment by moment. Practice often, and never give up. (It's worth mentioning here that while it is never too early to start training your Shepherd, it is also never too late.)

Who's responsible

Anyone and everyone in your puppy's close and extended family – and all using the same spoken commands, hand signals and body language.

Where?

Start training in a quiet place with no outside distractions. A closed room is infinitely better than a park with other puppies play-fighting nearby.

What?

By the time he is six months old, your puppy should know his name and obey your orders to: 'Come', 'Sit' and 'Down'. He should also have been introduced to 'Stay'.

How?

All commands should be spoken clearly, firmly and with confidence. At least initially, lengthen the vowel sounds and make sure the consonants are clear.

Your voice and treats are key to training your puppy, but don't forget about gestures. Most dogs actually respond better to body language than to words.

Name Recognition

One of the first things your puppy needs to learn is to recognise his name. After all, how else will he know that you're communicating with him?

Do

- From a short distance – three or four feet is fine – call your puppy clearly, using his name just once.
- Use a happy, friendly voice.
- Crouch down if you can.
- Open your arms to welcome him (body language is hugely important).
- Make a fuss of him when he gets to you.
- If he doesn't respond, wait a few seconds then call again, still clearly, and still just the once.
- When he does come, praise him lovingly, give him a small treat and tell him how brilliantly clever he is.
- Practise this often.

Don't

- Overuse his name or say it repeatedly in quick succession, or he will soon learn to ignore it.

EYE CONTACT

If your puppy is not looking at you, he is probably not listening either. Calling his name will encourage him to look at you and, when he does, you can know he's engaged. He's turning to you to find out what's coming next: will you open the door, take him for a walk, throw the ball? It's excellent that he's turning to you for answers and provision, so make sure you reward him.

CALLING HIM TO YOU

If your dog only knows one command it should be 'Come' or 'Here'. Coming to you when he's called is important for your relationship, and essential for his safety too. Recall is much like the name recognition exercise and now, while he is little, is a very good time to teach it to him because this is when he needs you more than ever for love, food and safety. In fact, if he's already joined your family, chances are he is with you right now, under your feet or helping you to absorb this book. Digest it even. And chances are he already relates the recall command to something fun and exciting: food, a new toy or play time.

Do

- Follow the steps in the Name Recognition exercise above, using his name and adding a calling word like 'Come' or 'Here'. Consistency is key, so choose which word you prefer and stick with it.
- Call him to you often, gradually increasing the initial distance between you.
- Practice at home and on a lead before you let him go when you are out and about.

- When you do let him off the lead away from home, make sure it is in a very safe place. Then practise letting him go and calling him back.
- If he keeps following you anyway, find someone who can help you by holding him while you back away. Then entice him, if necessary, and when he is struggling to get to you, your helper can let him go. Only then, when he is running to you, call his name and 'Come' or 'Here'.
- Your welcoming body language can be very helpful with this too. Try getting down on your knees and opening your arms wide to greet him.

Don't

- If you call your dog to you and he gets side-tracked en route, you might be tempted to scold him when he finally arrives. But coming to you should ALWAYS be associated with good things, so never punish him if he doesn't come straight away. If you do, he'll associate the scolding with the last thing he's done – come to you. Then, understandably from his point of view, he'll think twice the next time about coming back at all. (See 'Timing is all-important' in the chapter on Behaviour.)
- Don't **always** put him back on a lead when he comes to you, or he will soon learn that coming means the end of his free-play session. Only put him back on the lead after several recalls.

TIP
If he develops the habit of running up to you
but then dancing around just out of your reach,
start withholding his treat until AFTER
you have a grip on his collar.

'SIT'

This is one of the most useful exercises you can teach your puppy.

- Call him to you and hold a treat, palm facing down, just in front of his nose for him to smell.
- When you've got his interest, slowly take the treat up a couple of inches and over his head (slightly behind and above his eyes).

- When he lowers his bottom, say 'Sit!' and give him the treat.
- Once he is doing this well, you can move on to the next stage. Wait until his bottom is actually on the floor before you say 'Sit!', and only then give him the treat.
- He will soon learn to associate the word with the action. In time you can teach him to sit for longer stretches, from further away and during distractions.

NOTE
German Shepherds are excellent with words so be careful not to ask him to 'Sit down!' if you only want him to 'Sit!', because once he has learned the 'Down!' command as well, he won't know whether you're asking for a 'Sit' or a 'Down'

'DOWN'

- It is best to start teaching this command when your puppy is already in an attentive sit.
- Without feeding him the treat in your hand, move your hand, still palm down, from above his nose and towards the floor, between his front paws and close to his body.
- When he lowers his nose and front paws, keeping his bottom on the ground, say 'Down!' in a clear voice and give him the treat.
- When he is doing this well, you can wait until his tummy and all four paws are flat on the floor before you say 'Down!', and only then give him the treat.

'STAY'

This is an essential command for the safety or your puppy – or any dog that would otherwise dash out the front door, across a road, or leap out of the car.

The training involves teaching him to remain in a Sit or Down position for increasingly long times before you reward him.

- Once he is in a 'Sit' or a 'Down', say 'Stay!' in a strong but soothing voice, and combine this with a clear hand signal. With your arm straight, your palm flat and your fingers together, point to the ground just in front of him.
- If he gets up, simply ask for the Sit or Down position again and repeat the 'Stay' command.
- When he has stayed for a few seconds, say 'Good!' (or another 'release' word of your choice) and give him a treat.
- Gradually work up to longer times, but no more than 30 seconds, and step back in increments to increase the distance. (There's no point giving him unrealistic goals, so the idea is to push him to the limit while letting him succeed.)
- Keep him on a lead when you put this command into practice at the front door or in the car.

What if the training's 'not working'?

If your puppy doesn't do what you've asked (assuming he's not hard of hearing):

- he doesn't understand and needs clearer instructions,
- he needs more practice,
- or he needs a better reason to obey you – like a treat, an even better treat, or higher praise.

EXPANDING ON THE BASICS

Extension exercises

Duration – Once your puppy can do an exercise, like 'Sit' for example, you can gradually ask him to sit for longer periods before treating him.

Distractions – You can slowly increase the distractions too. A 'Sit' when a squirrel is taunting your puppy from a nearby tree is very different from a 'Sit' in a quiet place. Once he's mastered the instruction in a quiet room, start practising it in a busier part of the house, then at the park, then on a street corner, and so on.

Distance – In time, you can also begin asking your puppy to 'Sit' from slightly further away from you, but start with just a couple of steps and don't forget the all-important hand signals.

Advanced commands – If you'd like to add to these basic commands, your puppy can go on to learn 'Stand', 'Settle', 'Heel' and many more. There are some excellent obedience training books on the market, and if training classes are available in your area, they are well worth the effort and your dog would absolutely love you for taking him.

25. PLAYTIME!

Playing with your puppy helps to develop his socialising, improve his communication skills, and give him the mental and physical exercise German Shepherds so badly need. Most importantly of all, it's great fun. But whether you're just messing around or trying something more structured, you should always keep these Rules of Play top of mind.

- Start playtimes when your puppy's being good, so you're not rewarding him for bad behaviour.
- Several short play sessions spread throughout the day are always better than one long one.
- Whatever games you're playing, remember he's only little, so don't overpower him. Be sure to match your strength, speed and energy to his own.
- As far as possible, get down low to his level (small children excepted).
- If a toy is involved, avoid hard tugging. Never let his feet leave the ground as he clings to a toy. It puts too much pressure on his teeth, and encourages more aggressive play. Holding the toy by your fingertips is a good way to manage the pressure.
- When your puppy wins the toy, encourage him back to teach him that playing is more about having fun together than possession.

- If the playing does shift from fun interaction to possession of a toy, then stop for a while.
- Always try to calm the playing down before you stop. It's disappointing stopping a game when it's at its most exciting.
- And always end playtime on a good note. If you've had to stop for a moment, restart the game and end it when things are quiet and friendly.

For playtime to be great fun, you just need each other – there's no need for fancy toys or expensive equipment. Sharing a walk, throwing a ball and paddling in the shallows can be the most special times. But if you're still looking to expand your activities and further enrich your time together, here are some ideas.

GAMES

All puppies have their favourites and you will soon figure out which ones you play best together.

Chase

This game is excellent practice for encouraging your puppy to come to you when he is older.

1. Flick a treat across the floor.

2. Let him chase after it.

3. When he comes back for more, make eye contact and praise him.

4. Only then flick another treat across the floor, and so on.

Fetch

This is an extension of Chase, but outside or in a much bigger space.

1. Throw things for him to fetch: toys, a ball, a treat.

2. Say 'Fetch!' as you throw each item.

3. Once he knows to fetch, start throwing the objects into harder-to-reach places.

4. If this doesn't work, throw more interesting toys or tastier treats.

Catch

You can play this with toys, treats and balls.

1. Start with something light and easy to grab hold of, like a floppy soft toy.

2. Throw it in an arc over his head, so that if he stayed in place it would land close to his muzzle.

3. If he misses, try to pick it up before him and he will soon learn that if he wants it he must catch it before it hits the ground.

4. When he's learned to catch, you can move on to balls as well. (Much later he can progress to frisbees which are even more challenging, but be sure to start with a soft disc.)

Which hand?

1. With your hands behind your back, put a small treat or two in one hand and nothing in the other.

2. Make your hands into fists and bring them in front of you.

3. Let your puppy choose which fist he prefers the smell of.

4. When he's decided which hand he's interested in, and it's the right one, say 'Good!' and open your hand, letting him take the treat.

Treasure hunt

Your puppy will love this! German Shepherds are excellent at sniffing things out and relish any opportunity to put their skill to the test. What's more, rooting around for hidden treasure can be played just as well indoors as out.

1. The first time you play, let him follow you and watch as you hide a treat (something he can eat), then lead him away and say 'Find'.

2. As a next step, you could ask someone to hold him while he watches you hide the treat. When you get back to him, you can let him 'Find'.

3. Once he understands how the game works, you can make sure he can't see you at all when you hide the treat or a toy. Then lead him into the room or area of the garden where it's hidden, say 'Find', and this time he will have to follow your smell. (The first few times you might need to guide him.)

One day, when he is older, well trained and fully understands the game, you can make it more difficult by using 'Sit!' and 'Stay!' while you hide the treat, and then by hiding it in more difficult places too.

The memory game

When your puppy is a little older and has mastered some easy games, you can move on to more difficult challenges, like this one.

1. Put a treat in a sealed box or bag (because we want him to remember where it is rather than sniffing it out) and let him watch while you hide it.

2. Lead him away and distract him (for no more than 30 seconds at first).

3. Then say
'Where is it?', and initially
you might need to guide him.

4. When he understands how the game works, you
can make the distraction time longer and longer.

Obstacle course

1. Turn your passageway or garden into an obstacle
   course – build jumps, make tunnels, fill a tea tray
   with water, arrange boxes to navigate around …
   anything you can think of that is safe.

2. Guide your puppy through the course and reward
   him with treats each time he overcomes an
   obstacle.

TOYS

To keep your puppy interested in his toys, don't put them all out at the same time. Only let him play with or chew a few at a time, and rotate them during the day or through the week.

Presumably he'll have a range of toys that roll, bounce or squeak – toys that are wonderfully chewy or simply soft and cuddly. But here are three ideas for playtime that are a little more interesting and challenging.

The maze

There are a number of 'slow feeder' pet toys on the market which are maze-like in design. They are intended for dogs who gulp their food down too fast, but they also work brilliantly for brain-training.

- Put a treat or two in the middle and let him use his paws, snout and tongue to work the treats out of the maze before he can eat them.

The hollow chew

Hollow toys made of hard rubber, the Kong for example, are available online and from most pet stores. Fill one of these with small dog treats, or even with peanut butter (as long as it contains no Xylitol), or marmite if you can get hold of it. Your dog will spend hours trying to crunch or lick out whatever you've filled it up with.

Activity balls

There are plenty of these on the market in a range of shapes and sizes. Put dry food or treats inside one of these and your puppy will love rolling it around to get the pieces out.

EQUIPMENT

Use your imagination, but make sure whatever you come up with is safe, and well secured where necessary.

- Hay bales can be used as jumps, steps and passageways
- Old tires make fabulous jump hoops
- Children's paddling pools are great fun for playing in as well as cooling off in on hot days
- Look in children's toy stores – tunnels, playhouses and sand boxes will appeal to your puppy too.

26. TRAVELLING BY CAR

Of course your German Shepherd would love nothing more than to stand on the front passenger seat, stick his head out the window and feel the wind in his face, but car travel is not the time for free play.

Ideally you should invest in one of the following, depending on whether you want your dog to travel on the back seats, or – if your car has a rear door – in the space behind the back seats.

- a seatbelt harness – well-padded and comfortable, that fastens securely into your vehicle's existing seatbelt fitting,
- a crate or cage that is small enough to fit in the back area of your car while also being big enough for your adult dog to sit up and have a stretch in,
- a dog guard – fitted between the back seats of your car and the trunk/boot area.

All of these are available in pet stores and online.

Never
- Get him into or out of the car on the traffic side of the road.
- Allow your puppy or dog on your lap while you're driving.
- Allow him on the front passenger seat, especially if an airbag is fitted.

- Tie him in place on the back seat by his collar and lead instead of using a proper seatbelt harness.
- Leave him strapped into the car in the blaring sunlight. This would hurt him just as much as it would you.
- Leave him unattended in a hot or even warm car for more than five minutes. Dog fatalities from heatstroke in cars are frighteningly common.

Do

- Whenever you are getting your dog into the car or letting him out, make sure it is on the pavement side of the road.
- For everyone's safety, use a doggy seatbelt, crate or cage, or dog guard.
- For his own safety, teach him to 'Stay!' in the car until he is given the command to exit.
- On long journeys, stop regularly to let him relieve himself and stretch his legs. These stops will also help ease any car sickness he might experience.

27. PUPPY-PEOPLE TRANSLATOR

Your dog understands your every word, or so it's said. The point is, your choice of words is very important. Even more important though is **how** you say them. Be clear in your body language and be gentle but firm, patient, loving, encouraging, reassuring.

It is also said that a dog can say more with his tail in just a few seconds than his owner can say in hours. If he's already in your life, you will be familiar with his favourite expressions: 'I am so happy to see you!' and 'You are the best thing that ever happened to me!'. In his earliest days with you, you will no doubt have braced yourself for, 'Your face is like a lovely lolly!' And before long – but only if you've been 'good' – you could be surprised by another frequent favourite: 'Your training is coming along very nicely!'.

Yup, a lot of your puppy's body language is really easy to read, but truth be told the signs are not always straightforward. How good are you really at understanding his language? By way of example, a wagging tail can be a sign of happiness as well as one of aggression, so we need to look at the whole picture including: how he wags it, what the rest of his body is doing at the time and what else is going on around him.

To help with this, here are some English–German Shepherd translations:

I love you
- Racing to meet you
- Wagging tail
- Licking
- Whimpering

I'm happy and excited
- Tail wagging fast (but watch out as this can also be a sign of concentration or aggression)
- Racing around
- Whimpering
- Pulling lips back and exposing teeth

Let's play
- Wagging tail vigorously
- Rolling head
- Dashing off and jumping back again
- Jumping in front of you, facing you, front legs splayed out
- Elbows on the ground and bottom in the air (the play-bow)
- Bounding leaps
- Running in circles
- Lying down or rolling over
- Barking intermingled with growls (can be confused with aggression)

What is that I hear? Where is it coming from?
- One paw raised
- Head tilted to the side
- Brow raised
- Ears twitch and nose wiggles
- Mouth may be open and panting

Totally chilled out
- Lying on back with legs flopped out
- Curled in a ball
- Lying down watching you

Feeling submissive
- Rolling over onto back, exposing tummy and genitals
- Tail between legs
- Head dipped or tucked in, ears pinned back

**I'm curious, and maybe
a little concerned, about
something going
on out there**   - Raised paw

**I'm frightened
or unhappy**   - Tail between legs
- Cowering, or lying down
- Ears twitching back and forth
- Staring ahead at object of fear
- Lying down with paws ahead,
  looking ahead, ready to run
- Raised hackles (hairs along the top
  of his back)
- Whining
- Whimpering
- Looking to you for help

**I'm in pain or
frightened and
want your help**   - Looking from you to whatever it is
  he needs, and then quickly back
  again
- Whining or whimpering
*This is not manipulation. It's a genuine plea for help.
Tell him you're there for him and he can count on you.*

Aggressive   - Standing up straight
- Ears pinned back, or sharply
  forward
- Hackles raised
- Low growl with eyes fixed in a
  direct stare

- Body is tense, ready to attack
- Tail held stiffly, or wagging in stiff, quick, stilted movements
- Barking
- Sudden unpredictable bites
- Growling or biting (as a response to punishment or in defence of food or toys)

I'm warning you
- Snarling
- Growling
- Baring fangs

Feeling lonely and locating other dogs, or sending out a warning
- Howling
- Baying

I want your attention: 'hello', 'look at me', 'I'm bored'
- Barking directly at you

I'm begging you. Pleeez!
- Whining, with pleading eyes

Yes, it's a heart-wrenching expression, but don't give in to that cute little face. Your environment will help you to tell the difference between manipulative begging and 'I'm in pain or frightened and need your help'. If you're eating a juicy steak that he's hoping you'll share, it's safe to assume he's begging.

28. GOING FORWARD

Somewhere between five months and a year your puppy will go through adolescence, which is usually the most difficult period for owners. He is growing in independence; his chewing continues relentlessly; and he will become more territorial. Hopefully the solid foundations you've laid in the early weeks and months will make this stage a little less wearing. Remind yourself it is short-lived.

Your puppy is also beginning to show the onset of sexual maturity and is likely to go off exploring because she or he wants to mate. Females will come into season and be overcome with the urge to roam, and males will begin mounting things, marking their territory and maybe even fighting with other male dogs. Both sexes will experience hormonal changes that are likely to affect their behaviour, so if you're not planning on breeding, then having your dog neutered (castrated or spayed) can be the answer to the problem.

Neutering

Early neutering in German Shepherds has been found to increase the risk of joint disorders as well as other health problems, and it is commonly agreed that they shouldn't be neutered until well after a year. An in-depth study by Benjamin Hart – conducted specifically to determine the best time for German Shepherds to be neutered – concluded that a suitably safe age is between 16 and 18 months.

This said, the best time for neutering always varies from dog to dog as well as from breed to breed. This is because it's important to get the balance right between physical growth and emotional maturity. The average German Shepherd will reach its full frame size between 15 months and two years of age, though some Eastern European lines can take up to three years. Emotional maturity is more difficult to pinpoint, but less bounce and reduced chewing are both good indicators.

Running off

If your adolescent puppy starts running off – most likely because he wants to mate – and this behaviour persists, prevention is always the better option. At home you will need to keep him inside or in a fully-enclosed garden or yard, and while walking out he will need to stay on the lead.

But if he does run off (or away), be sure to praise him when he comes back (or home). Never scold him when he gets to you, because in coming back he is being a good puppy. That way he will want to stay with you (or home) and, even if he does run off again, he will always want to return.

The special place

When your puppy is toilet trained and has stopped eating everything in sight, you will be able to start leaving the door to his crate or special space open. In the meantime, remember to keep praising him when you see him going in there on his own.

Feeding

Between nine months and a year old you will also be able to cut your puppy's feeds back from three times to twice a day. At around a year you can move him on to adult food.

Nails

If you can hear your German Shepherd's nails clacking on the floor, they need trimming. Apart from being uncomfortable, nails that are too long can cause splayed feet and lameness. And if the dewclaws (the claws higher up on the wrists) get too long, they can get caught on things, ripped out, or even start growing into the skin.

Fine tuning

This book sets out to answer the most important early-stage questions on owning a German Shepherd puppy. It covers the things you need to know when he is still very young – the things you don't want to get wrong in his vital first months.

At a later stage you might well choose to fine-tune your training, or need to deal with specific behavioural issues that could've arisen. There are some excellent and extremely thorough books on the market. And if you've got the time and inclination for obedience training classes, they are incredibly enriching for both you and your dog. He would love you for taking him, forever and more.

29. STANDOUT GERMAN SHEPHERDS

STRONGHEART

Strongheart was trained as a police dog before serving in the German Red Cross in World War I. His owner was left in poverty after the war and sent him, aged three, to New York to be sold. There, film director Laurence Trimble recognised his potential and directed him in four rugged outdoor adventure films including White Fang (1925). Strongheart became the first major canine film star, preceding the fame of Rin Tin Tin by two years.

RIN TIN TIN

This most famous of Shepherds was rescued from a World War I battlefield by an American soldier who found him work in silent films. He was an immediate box-office success and went on to appear in 27 Hollywood films, gaining worldwide fame and boosting the success of Warner Bro. Studio. Together with Strongheart, he was responsible for a rapid increase in the popularity of the breed as family pets.

CRUMSTONE IRMA

Irma helped in the rescue of 191 people who were trapped under blitzed buildings in London during

World War II. She was noted for her ability to tell if buried victims were dead or alive, and to communicate this to her handlers with different barks. When Irma signalled an 'alive' bark, and rescuers dug out a victim they declared 'dead', Irma was proved correct, as the victim eventually stirred. Irma refused to give up on the scent of two girls who were trapped under a fallen building for two days. In 1945, she was awarded the Dickin Medal, the animals' equivalent of the Victoria Cross.

CRUMSTONE PSYCHE

Initially used to relay messages when telephone lines were down, Psyche was retrained as a search and rescue dog and teamed with Irma. With their handler, Margaret Griffin, they found 233 people, of which 21 were found alive.

JET OF IADA

Jet assisted in the rescue of 150 people trapped under London's blitzed buildings during World War II. He was awarded both the Dickin Medal and the RSPCA's Medallion of Valour for his contribution.

APPOLLO

The first search and rescue dog on the scene after the September 11 attacks on the World Trade Center, Appollo was almost killed by flames and falling debris but, having fallen into a pool of water just moments before, he survived and started working again as soon as his handler, Peter Davis, had brushed the debris off him. He too was awarded the Dickin Medal, in recognition of the work done by all search and rescue dogs following the fall of the Twin Towers.

Gallantry and devotion to duty

So many noteworthy dogs are credits to this already credit-worthy breed – far too many for the confines of this book. Suffice it to say that to date, two-thirds of all dogs awarded the Dicken Medal for gallantry and devotion to duty are German Shepherds.

YOURS TRULY [_____]

Because I know you have invited a very special
German Shepherd into your home – a puppy that is
already heroic in its own right.

30. THERE WILL BE TIMES ...

This book is intended as an easy read to offer you some shortcuts with the theory. But there are NO shortcuts with the practice. The practice needs patience and repetition, encouragement and reward.

Tough times

There will be times when your puppy does all sorts of things you don't want him to. When he's bored and teething, he will set his alligator jaws to work, chomping their happy way through your designer

chairs. He will slop his muddy paws across your cream-coloured carpet, then wait until he's well and truly indoors before shaking off the rest of the muck. He will gift you with shredded items of now ex-value, and random deposits of unidentifiable bodily waste.

He will bark when he has something to say, and whine when he's upset or lonely. For months, your house will be littered with toys, and the tick-tack of determined paws will be under your feet when you go to the fridge, the toilet, the shower and the front door.

There are many times when you will be at your wits' end and you will look at him and think, 'What have I got myself into?'

Well it's this: when he is fully grown, he will distribute his fur generously, far and wide. He will take up space on your bed, sofa, passage floor and entrance area. In fact, wherever he is allowed you will be navigating your way around him. He will need so much exercise that you'll struggle to keep up. He will bark at strangers, and decide who should be allowed to visit. And if you aren't firm enough with the rules, your new family member will soon be ruling the house.

But it's precisely because they are big and brave and furry that we love them; because they are heroic, energetic and need loads of stimulation. So, remember that when you feel your patience running thin, and don't try to make him more human.

Good times

Just as he is, you will have more love and more fun than you could ever imagine, and there will be many times when you ask yourself, 'How did I get so lucky?'.

Your family has grown by four furry feet and when you get home, your new best friend is waiting to greet you, ecstatic to see you. He will enrich your life with his unconditional love and loyalty, gratitude and forgiveness, help and protection, and buckets and buckets of laughs.

There will also be plenty of times when he does the things you DO want him to do. Praise him – with attention, treats, toys … it doesn't matter what, as long as it's something he loves.

Taking-him-for-granted times

And last, but definitely not least, there will be times when he just IS – a calm, quiet presence by your side. Those are the times when it will be easiest for you to forget or ignore him, and those are the times when it is most important of all to remind yourself, and him, just how special he is. As the saying goes, "Everyone has a guardian angel. The lucky ones have a German Shepherd."

31. USEFUL CONTACTS

Websites

American Kennel Club
www.akc.org/dog-breeds/german-shepherd-dog

Animal Health Trust
www.aht.org.uk

Australian National Kennel Council
ankc.org.au/breed/detail/158

Company of Animals
Companyofanimals.co.uk

German Shepherd Dog Club of America (GSDCA)
gsdca.org

German Shepherd Dog (Alsatian) Club of the UK
gsdalsatianclubuk.org.uk

Kennel Union of Southern Africa
www.kusa.co.za

The Dog Training Secret.com
thedogtrainingsecret.com

The German Shepherd Dog League of Great Britain
www.gsdleague.co.uk

The Kennel Club (UK)
www.thekennelclub.org.uk

Total German Shepherd
total-german-shepherd.com

United Schutzhund Clubs of America (for
American breeders with dogs from European lines)
www.germanshepherddog.com

White Shepherd Dog Club International, Inc.
www.whitegermanshepherd.org

INDEX